BEST
TAROT
PRACTICES

BEST
TAROT
PRACTICES

Everything You Need to Know to Learn the Tarot

MARCIA MASINO

FOREWORD BY
RACHEL POLLACK

WEISERBOOKS
San Francisco, CA / Newburyport, MA

First published in 2009 by
Red Wheel/Weiser, LLC
With offices at:
500 Third Street, Suite 230
San Francisco, CA 94107
www.redwheelweiser.com

ISBN: 978-1-57863-432-3
Library of Congress Cataloging-in-Publication Data is available on request.

Cover and text design by Kathryn Sky-Peck.
Author photo © Edie

Printed in Canada
TCP
10 9 8 7 6 5 4 3 2 1
The paper used in this publication meets the minimum requirements of the American
National Standard for Information Sciences—Permanence of Paper for Printed Library
Materials Z39.48-1992 (R1997).

For the Light Workers of the Tarot.

TABLE OF CONTENTS

Part One:
The Reader and the Tarot

Part Two:
Three New Tarot Spreads

Part Three: New Meanings
& Meditations for the Major Arcana

Part Four: New Meanings & Meditations for the Minor Arcana

FOREWORD

Rachel Pollack

My first experience with this book came well before reading it. It was at the Reader's Studio, a yearly conference in the New York area that has become a major event for Tarot people around the world. Marcia was one of three presenters, and gave us a fascinating way to look at the Minor Arcana in the famous Rider deck of A. E. Waite and P. C. Smith (the one that first put action scenes on all the cards). She identified each suit with a medieval virtue and proceeded to show how each card in that suit, each scene, could be seen as either a triumph of that virtue or a test of its basic quality. I found this not only an exciting idea but a good method to explore what we see in the pictures beyond the usual ways we have learned to look at them.

Consider the suit of Pentacles, which Marcia aligns with the virtue of Charity. Since the original symbol for the suit was Coins, this makes sense. Two cards would seem obvious. In the Four we see a crowned man scowling as he holds tight to one large Pentacle, with two others under his feet, and the fourth on top of his head. Clearly this forms a test (not to say, failure) of Charity, for this fellow wants to keep all his riches for himself.

But what of the Six? There we see a merchant (or as Dr. Waite mysteriously put it, "a man in the guise of a merchant") giving a few coins to a beggar on his knees while a second beggar waits his turn. Since the picture shows the very act of Charity, it would seem a clear triumph. Or is it? When I brought Marcia's approach back to my monthly class in upstate New York, we found there were many ways to look at this card. Maybe it was a test because the poor people had to get down on their knees and beg before the rich fellow would give them anything. Or maybe this was part of the triumph, for learning how to get on our knees and ask for help can be one of life's most valuable lessons, possibly more important than the actual coins. And so the discussion went, with Marcia's concept allowing us to see each card in a fresh way.

This alone is a great "virtue" in the Tarot world, for it is far too easy to decide that we know exactly what a card means, and thus give up really looking at it. I also like the virtue idea because it helps return Tarot to its roots, as an expression of the early Renaissance.

Best Tarot Practices is a very modern book, with a whole slew of exercises and ideas not just for learning the Tarot but for using it in our lives. At the same time, Marcia knows deeply the Tarot's tradition of esoteric ideas as well as the world of its origins. I like her description of the Tarot as a "metaphysical vessel." As she says, we can "divine" the soul externally through readings, and experience it inwardly through meditation.

This is a useful book, and that alone is a virtue. As well as giving us meanings and spreads and techniques, Marcia takes up such issues as the difference between fortune-telling and helping people take responsibility for their lives, or what to do when psychic information comes through in a reading. None of these qualities or approaches are right in every moment; we need to learn to identify them, balance them, and know when to use them. She approaches such important subjects as how to phrase "bad news," if that comes up in a reading. She also discusses a vital issue that many Tarot readers simply will not consider—that the cards are "not always correct."

And yet, Marcia's thorough background in the Tarot's esoteric traditions underlies all this practical advice. For example, she mentions as an aside that the falcon or hawk on the Nine of Pentacles is an "icon" of Tarot because it represents the Egyptian god Horus "who presides over the cards." She goes on to give us Aleister Crowley's invocation of the guardian angel of the cards, Uriel, whose name means Light of God. She also mentions that the card of the Hermit signifies Uriel, presumably for the lantern he holds up. These asides also give the cards greater dimension.

Unlike many Tarot books, *Best Tarot Practices* moves beyond theory and lists of meanings, and even exercises, to suggest ways we can bring the Tarot alive. One of my favorites involves a scavenger hunt. She suggests that readers take a digital camera and go out and photograph images that in some way evoke particular Tarot cards. This delightful exercise not only tests our knowledge of the cards but also pushes us to go beyond concepts to a living experience.

She suggests as well the idea of a costume party (always fun— I remember at a convention once, a woman came to the Saturday evening costume party with bras pinned all over her dress; she was, of course, the Queen of Cups), but perhaps more interesting, finding everyday clothes that evoke a card you wish to bring alive. It's one thing to dress up as the High Priestess for a party of like-minded friends, but what would you wear to work that somehow kept you connected to that card if it was important in your life right now? She suggests using colors, jewelry, even kinds of clothing (for example, long dresses vs. trousers) to express the card. This is a great suggestion, even if you don't do it all the time, for all of us face situations where we would like to evoke a particular card.

Marcia also recommends that we do certain things or go places to bring a card alive. One of my favorites is the suggestion to evoke the Tower by going to a demolition derby. I think I can safely say this is the first time I've seen this idea in any Tarot book. Such things get us thinking in new ways. I can imagine a class project to build a Tower and then smash it to bits.

For all its down-to-earth qualities this book does not lose sight of the Tarot's spiritual side. Unlike many Tarot texts it does not give us the particular card-by-card meanings until after she offers these varied ways to approach the cards. When Marcia does give us meanings, she includes esoteric meanings, meditations of various sorts (I like that they are not all the same), questions we might ask ourselves, and affirmations.

Best Tarot Practices is a useful book, a practical book, in the truest fashion, to be of aid on many levels, and in a whole range of practices.

INTRODUCTION

*B*est *Tarot Practices* provides everything you need to know to read cards for personal insight and spiritual growth. The book, dedicated to the Tarot reader, tackles all aspects of Tarot interpretation, making it a great resource guide. You'll discover interesting information about surprising subjects, like how to determine the way your psychic ability functions when reading the cards. The book guides readers through challenging situations, and offers simple new streamlined card interpretations to try. You'll explore unconventional ways to learn the cards' meanings, and discover the joys of Tarot reading and how it can help you to develop spiritually. Reading *Best Tarot Practices* is like having an expert teaching you the best Tarot techniques in the comfort of your own home.

My first book, *Easy Tarot Guide,* has been in print for over twenty years. It has sold well over 100,000 copies and has been translated into many languages. I have filled this new book with the best Tarot methods based on my thirty years as a professional reader, author, educator, and Certified Grandmaster of Tarot.

Best Tarot Practices is dedicated to Tarot readers and their experiences with the cards. The quotes on page 301 are from Tarot interpreters throughout the world. Their comments serve as testimony to the vast variety of experiences and benefits derived from card reading.

The situations that a Tarot reader encounters—social scenarios, challenging readings, and difficult cards—are a main feature of this book. Its interactive workbook style will help you learn the "how to" of Tarot interpretation through learning tools and examples that explain the integration of cards with their layout placements. These explanations of the cards are supplemented by new, focused, easy-to-learn card meanings. We'll also address some unexpected subjects in great detail, like how to determine how your psychic ability is involved during a session, how to acquire reading experience, how to use unconventional methods for learning the cards, and how to pursue spiritual development through the Tarot.

The person who consults the cards asking for a forecast or self-awareness is known as the Seeker. In a sense, we all are Seekers; we look to the Tarot for predictions and for guidance for ourselves, for family and friends, and for clients and fellow students. I regard the deck as a lifelong companion that can gradually reveal my destiny over time.

I believe the Tarot's genius is its unique ability to blend the mystical with the practical through visual symbols. The symbolism of the cards illustrates the lessons and blueprint of the soul divined externally through readings and experienced inwardly through meditation. This is the greatest gift the Tarot offers humankind.

When you study the Tarot, you become a custodian of an ancient knowledge that neither begins nor ends with you. Reading Tarot in the best possible way opens the door to the treasures of prophecy, spiritual understanding, and life progression through applied wisdom. The techniques, examples, and learning tools in *Best Tarot Practices* will provide you with the best practical and spiritual ways to interpret and utilize the knowledge offered by the remarkable metaphysical vessel known as the Tarot.

PART ONE

THE READER
AND THE TAROT

Best Tarot Practices is dedicated to all Tarot readers. I believe that reading the cards is a unique experience for each reader, but at the same time some common situations do occur. My intention is to address them through guidance and shared experience. I want to introduce new ways of perceiving how the cards' energies are already operating within and through you as healers, guides, sources of spiritual education, and forces of transformation.

• 1 •

MASTERING CARD MEANINGS

A repertoire of memorable, clear card interpretations is vital to a successful Tarot reading. Students often remark that some of the cards' meanings remain elusive for them. Although initially you may think that you will become an expert reader by learning many meanings for each card, this can backfire on you at the worst possible moment—during a session—if you are not certain which interpretation to use!

I feel that having a simple effective description for every card boils down to a few carefully chosen words. All you need to grasp the interpretative message of each card is an easy-to-remember key phrase that makes sense to you. Once you've devised an unforgettable meaning for each card, you can relax and allow the interpretive "flow" of the reading's message to unfold. This open, receptive state fosters psychic promptings and inspired interpretations of the card messages.

Later, you can add more meanings and even a spiritual component to your Tarot readings. For now, let's aim for simplicity and clarity.

THE FOUR SUITS

Begin by selecting the cards you want to master from your deck and dividing them into two piles—the Major and the Minor Arcana. Then separate the Minor cards into the four suits and place any Court cards you've chosen aside for attention later.

Step 1: Developing Keywords

Keywords provide an easy way to master card meanings. My new streamlined themes for the Minor Arcana suits can be integrated easily into your Tarot repertoire. They are based on the classical affiliation between the four suits and the four medieval virtues of fortitude, faith, justice, and charity.

Wands indicate fortitude, courage, will, authenticity, and aspiration.

Cups denote faith, imagination, and love.

Swords represent justice, actions and reactions based on fairness and integrity, truth, conflict, and the mind.

Pentacles represent charity, benefactors, labors of love, money, and security.

Write three keywords that resonate with you from my meanings, or create your own in the space provided:

Wands _____

Cups _____

Swords _____

Pentacles _____

Step 2: The Scene and Characters' Actions

Select a card from the pile you've chosen to learn and write down the card title and some keywords to describe the scene. For example, how does the atmosphere or environment in the card appear to you? Is it harmonious? Loving? Unstable? Active? Stagnant? Calm? Filled with strife? Combative?

Card title _____

Scene _____

Now focus on the character of the card and his or her actions, attitudes, and behaviors. Is there aggression? Is the character moving forward or backward, or does he or she seem stuck in the situation? Is the action in the card happy? Protective? Defensive? Unaware? Forward-looking? Mournful? Remember that the characters demonstrate and act out the attitude of the card's message.

Characters' actions _____

Step 3: Putting It Together

When you match your keyword suit meanings to the scene and action descriptions, you develop an interpretation that is memorable because you created it. For example, Kevin felt challenged when interpreting the Two of Swords. Following the steps I've outlined, he found a meaning that was memorable for him. Here is how he created it.

Kevin's keywords for the Sword suit were mind, truth, and actions. He then described the scene in the Two of Swords as calm, but tentative and uncertain. He felt as if the card showed pause and an action, behavior, and attitude of waiting. "I think I now have an interpretation I understand," said Kevin. He explained the Two of Swords easily in the following manner:

You are feeling undecided and unsure about your situation. You have chosen to wait calmly until more truthful, complete information is revealed to help you make up your mind.

This is a good, correct definition for the card. The Two of Swords indicated his quiet, wait-and-see, temporary stance or position. Remember, many Seekers consult the cards for advice during times of uncertainty and when they need clear information. The Two of Swords indicates this state of flux.

THE COURT CARDS

In this section, you'll learn new and effective ways to remember the meanings of the Court cards. My streamlined themes for each suit will help simplify your interpretations of these cards.

PAGE of WANDS.

KNIGHT of SWORDS.

QUEEN of CUPS.

KING of PENTACLES.

Step 1: Using Your Keywords

Place the Court cards you need to learn in front of you. Divide them into the four suits. Three basic words for each of the four suits are all you need for an accurate interpretation. These twelve words will be your keywords to apply to the Pages, Knights, Queens, and Kings.

Read the following descriptions of the character qualities, then write your own interpretation of them in the space provided, or choose the descriptions that are meaningful for you.

Wands: Clear likes and dislikes; extroverted, warm, strong, personable; leadership traits; values accomplishments; courageous, oriented toward achievement of goals and ideals. Now create your own keywords for the Wand Court cards or choose from those mentioned above.

1 _____

2 _____

3 _____

Cups: Intuitive, introspective, imaginative; interested in future possibilities; loving, nurturing, emotional, creative; powerful dreams; deep sustained faith. Now create your own keywords for the Cup Court cards, or choose from those mentioned above.

1 _____

2 _____

3 _____

Swords: Inquisitive, thoughtful; values the powers of the mind and learning; communicative; likes precise explanations; mind over matter; endeavors to treat self and others with fairness and integrity. Now create your own keywords for the Sword Court cards, or choose from those mentioned above.

1 _____

2 _____

3 _____

Pentacles: Practical, security-conscious, interested in building finances and career; hardworking, resourceful, capable, prosperous; realistic, methodical; feels strong connection with the earth and nature; charitable, labors lovingly and loves laboring toward valued goals. Now create your own keywords for the Pentacle Court cards, or choose from those mentioned above.

1 _____

2 _____

3 _____

You now have twelve keywords for the Court cards. Next, you'll use them to describe their characters.

Step 2: Techniques for Learning the Court Cards

My six techniques for learning the Court cards are:

- Descriptive storytelling
- Explaining or teaching to someone else
- Connecting word and picture
- Dreams

- Symbol and theme
- Association to family and friends

Decide which method feels compatible with your learning style.

• Descriptive Storytelling

If you enjoy storytelling, create a character-ization about the Court card you want to learn. Include character traits, motivation, and action. You can even relate the images to a favorite character from a film, television program, or novel.

For example, Lee decided he'd create a story characterization for the Page of Cups, a card he struggled to remember. His keywords for the suit of Cups were "emotional, family-oriented, and imaginative dreamer." The Page represents a youth, child, or baby.

PAGE of CUPS.

Lee then thought of a child with those character traits from the film world, one of his favorite subjects. Dorothy from *The Wizard of Oz* came to mind. She was emotional, sensitive, and attached to her family, and her story involved an imaginative dream. Dorothy easily represents the Page of Cups for Lee. Now, whenever this card appears in a reading, Lee describes the Page's character as a dreamer, a, sensitive, intuitive youth with an active imagination, deeply attached to family.

His new interpretation includes the emotional qualities of a sense of belonging and a need to be heard by family and loved ones, two other motivational traits he associates with Dorothy's character and her actions.

• Teaching and Explaining

This technique requires a study partner. It will reinforce your knowl-edge, and give you the experience of speaking your interpretation aloud to someone else. Hearing yourself speak will help you feel sure of your grasp of the card meaning.

Go through each Court card, explaining to your partner what you have learned about it. Invite your companion to ask questions about the card's character. Some examples of questions for your study partner to ask are:

QUEEN of PENTACLES

- If the Queen of Pentacles were a television drama character, who would she be?

- If the King of Cups were a singer, who would he be and why?

- If the Knight of Swords were an athlete, who would he be?

- How about the Queen of Wands as a politician?

Your explanation for your choices of character will help solidify your memory of the meaning.

KING of PENTACLES

• *Connecting Word and Picture*

If picture and word association appeals to you, use the keywords you have already chosen for a card's meaning for this study exercise. Select the Court card you want to learn. Now look at this card, imagining and associating the keywords to the various symbols, the scene, and the character.

For example, Jennifer's keywords for the suit of Pentacles were "conservative, realistic, and hardworking." The King and Knight of Pentacles were both challenging cards for her to interpret. She placed the two cards in front of her and then associated the keyword "realistic" with the picture of the Pentacle in the cards, a symbol for, among other things, money.

KNIGHT OF PENTACLES

"These men are realistic in financial matters," she said, noting the picture of the King's castle and the rich grape vines emphasized in his card. "The King has tangible property and knows how to build, cultivate, and maintain it using a dedicated work ethic and responsible attitude." Jennifer then looked at the Knight of Pentacles. Focusing on his horse, she arrived at the following interpretation:

> *The horse is a mode, way, or style of transportation taking the Knight where he wants to go. The horse in this card is obviously a strong workhorse, suggesting the down-to-earth conservative nature of the Knight's character as a hard worker. In other words, it represents how he attains his ambitions. The Knight is realistic about getting where he wants to go in life. He is able to move toward his goals, using a sensible plan.*

Jennifer now has a way to remember the two cards using picture and word associations. When she saw the various images, she simply applied her chosen words and her memory of this study exercise filled in the rest.

• *Dreams*

Another way to master a challenging card is to picture it while drifting into sleep. Choose a card that you want to learn, gaze at it before you fall asleep, and see it in your mind. Ask your subconscious to teach you a special meaning to help you remember the card. This may evoke a dream or personal memory that will instill and fix the interpretation into your consciousness.

QUEEN ʄ WANDS.

• Symbol and Theme

Learn one word for three aspects of a card. Look at the card and associate one word with its suit, one with its dominant color, and one with its character's action. Use the three words to create a key phrase that will help you interpret the card.

For example, Mark's challenging card was the Queen of Wands. His keywords for the suit of Wands were "radiant, enthusiastic, and powerful." He associated the word "enthusiastic" to the Queen's energetic blooming sunflower wand/suit. Then he applied the word "radiant" to the Queen herself, based on her sunny and warmly colored attire/dominant color. Mark described her as "comfortable" on her throne of power/character's main action. With each of his keywords now visually associated with her symbols, he can easily remember the meaning of the Queen of Wands:

> This woman is enthusiastic and radiant, and handles her powerful position with ease.

• Association to Family and Friends

Associating a character from your life to a card can help you remember its meaning. A Court card can remind you of a friend or family member. When you see the card, you can think of the character traits of that person.

You may also determine which Court card best represents your personality and apply that description in your reading. Consider which Page you would pick to represent your childhood. For example, were you outgoing (Wands), sensitive (Cups), inquisitive and curious (Swords),

PAGE ʄ SWORDS.

or nature-loving (Pentacles)? Remembering a Court card's meaning is easy when you associate it with a real person.

These six simple methods provide an effective way to master the meanings of the Court cards. By now you've probably realized that more than one can be effective for you and that the methods can also be applied to the Minor Arcana.

THE MAJOR ARCANA

This section focuses on the rich, detailed illustrations of the Major Arcana. These cards are carefully crafted to convey their message using symbolism. The meanings of the Major Arcana are easily learned once you know the secret: the vast variety of symbols often represents the one main theme of the card. Each symbol is a doorway into the card that leads to its essential meaning. The original designers of the deck felt that, if these symbols represented the same idea in a variety of ways, more people would be able to access the theme of the card.

For example, the meaning of the High Priestess is "remembering the soul." Each symbol in the card relates to the soul. Her scroll contains what is written in the soul's destiny. The white and black pillars represent that which has been and is yet to be written about the soul. Her veils conceal the soul. The water symbolizes the soul's vessel. The color blue represents soul energy. The sacred feminine—that is, the High Priestess herself—is a universal symbol for the divine aspect of the soul. As you can see, the main meaning of the card remains the same, "remembering the soul." The symbols are like many pathways, all leading to the same subject—in this example, the remembrance of the soul's content.

THE HIGH PRIESTESS

Mastering the Majors

Allow ample time for this exercise. Place one of the Major Arcana you wish to learn in front of you. Begin by scanning the card slowly from left to right, starting at the top, then moving to the middle, and ending at the bottom of the card. Write down the one feeling, color, action, or symbol that stands out for you after this scan. Next, write down some words that come to mind about the feature you've chosen.

Turn to the Major Arcana section on page 109 of this book. Read about your card and write down the words or phrases that help clarify, define, and enhance your interpretation. You now have your key phrase for the card linked with the symbol, feeling, color, or action that represents the meaning to you. Every time you see the card, your key phrase will pop into your mind.

For example, Maria felt unclear when interpreting the Judgement card. She set aside ample time for the scanning exercise, and discovered the outstanding symbol for her was the Archangel's horn. She wrote down the word "horn," and then associated the idea of sounding the trumpet. "I can hear it," she said. "Whenever I see that card, I hear the angel blowing the horn. It reminds me of an announcement—like an arrival, or an honor, or an achievement."

Then Maria asked herself what the characters in the card have achieved. For her, they have accomplished the cycle of life and are being called to heaven's gate. Therefore, this card represents to her an ending and a new beginning of a positive nature. She checked the meaning for Judgement and discovered her interpretation was absolutely valid. Now, when she sees the horn in the card, she hears it blow and remembers her key phrase of "a happy announcement of an achievement."

Ben chose new ways to interpret the Tower card. He had difficulty making sense of how it made him feel. "I actually experience a physical reaction when I see it," he said. "It gives me the chills. It feels so shocking, how can I express that to my clients? I need to find something helpful to say about it."

THE TOWER.

Using the scanning exercise, he discovered he was specifically drawn to the top of the Tower, with its falling structure and burning flames. "The card is so explosive," he commented. "It reminds me of a kind of holiday firework I had as a kid. It was called the 'Flaming Schoolhouse,' and consisted of a school building that burned down while shooting fiery sparks into the air. We loved it because it symbolized freedom from the rules and regulations of school." Ben now had a personal, positive meaning for the Tower card. His analogy perfectly fit with the card's stated interpretation of liberation from restrictions—both those we create ourselves and those created by others.

Emily is a practicing psychic who has been studying the cards and using them as part of her readings. "People seem to want me to include the cards during their sessions. That's OK with me. I feel very energized by the Tarot cards, and I'm able to get messages from them."

THE EMPEROR.

She felt challenged to come up with a clear interpretation for the Emperor card. I was intrigued that she was having trouble with one of the cards that actually represents her gift of clairvoyance. After the three scans, she declared, "I keep being drawn to his eyes. They seem so wise, clear, and compassionate. He makes me feel certain, secure, and reassured." Her description is accurate for the Emperor. He represents a masterful, protec-

15

tive, wise man with clear understanding and an ethical and moral compass. Emily now has her interpretation for the card. She uses the eyes as her memory trigger, calling them "wise eyes."

These examples show how quickly and easily you can learn the meanings of the Major Arcana. Don't be afraid to enhance book meanings with words and concepts that are relevant to you. Be open to new interpretations, especially those that feel pertinent and resonate with you.

They also illustrate the various psychic ways of receiving information in a Tarot reading. Maria heard the horn of Judgement's archangel; Ben physically felt the sensations of The Tower, describing them as shock and chills. Emily's experience with The Emperor was visual, in that she saw his eyes emote and communicate information.

The examples also represent the three types of intuition: clairaudience (hearing), clairsentience (feeling), and clairvoyance (seeing). Maria hears her intuitive messages; Ben senses and feels his; Emily sees hers. Observe how you receive impressions during your readings and meditations to determine your intuitive type. This will help you to be more aware of how psychic Tarot messages for yourself and others are already involved with your card interpretations.

Now that you feel confident with your new Tarot interpretations, we'll turn our attention to the best practices for applying them to a reading.

·2·

SUCCESSFUL
CARD INTERPRETATION

What good are the Tarot's messages if you cannot clearly discern and convey them? Understanding how the cards communicate and how their guidance is presented is paramount to successful card analysis. In this chapter, we'll explore the best interpretation techniques and tips for enhancing your reading style and determine how your psychic aptitude manifests when you are reading Tarot. Whether you are the Seeker asking the cards questions for yourself or reading for others, the information in this chapter will help you handle the many situations that inevitably arise about Tarot advising.

People often turn to the Tarot for advice about life areas where they are experiencing dissatisfaction of some kind. Wondering when life will become what they wish for, Seekers ask the cards for change. They usually want some form of transformation, but perceive it as being outside their control. Yet the solutions and clarity they desire often lie within, and it is the Tarot advisor's job to uncover and communicate those answers effectively.

This is where personal responsibility versus fortune and fate becomes important. You, as a reader, need to create a balance between predictions that forecast circumstances beyond the Seeker's control, and guidance about personal responsibility for change that comes from within that effect and interact with destiny. The cards usually indicate a subtle balance of both aspects, and a skilled reader can discern and interpret these messages with clarity and precision.

When consulting the Tarot for yourself, it is a good practice to ask a fellow Tarot reader for an opinion, since it is often difficult to be objective when pondering your own spread. Another way to access extra insight about the cards that appear is to read about them in your favorite Tarot books. Or you can explain the reading to someone else aware that, while you speak, supplementary messages will come to you.

I have been a professional Tarot reader and teacher since 1974 and have dealt extensively with the questions Seekers ask of the cards. The real difficulty is usually their inability to grasp their creative choices in a situation. In other words, they can't see beyond their insecurities and perceived powerlessness in order to help themselves. Another issue you'll face is reluctance on the part of Seekers to allow their power and gifts to bloom.

Some others cannot utilize the positive aspects of their lives for problem solving. For example, a Seeker may possess great discipline at work, yet not be able to apply it to tame a negative personal habit like smoking or overindulgence. You can point out that this person already possesses the necessary traits in one sphere of life and can choose to transfer those skills to the other sphere. This creates an empowered mindset and self-awareness.

You can help these Seekers to embrace their strengths. Encourage self-love and self-respect to help them solve their problems. A session that focuses on enhancing self-esteem and emphasizes how wonderful, deserving, and lovable they are can create a shift in consciousness. They may begin to feel less tense and more open to new possibilities and develop a sense of curiosity about the future, think more constructively, and act more productively. Essentially, you will have restored hope.

Here is an example of a reading that has a blend of negative and positive cards. It contrasts the strength derived from personal self-awareness and the fears and uncertainties that trouble us all. This combination of cards will often show up in a challenging situation. At first glance, in this example, the outcome card and the possible and immediate future cards all indicate a negative outcome to the Seeker's question about the future state of her marriage.

THE READING

Place the following cards in front of you in the Celtic Cross pattern as noted, and read my interpretations.

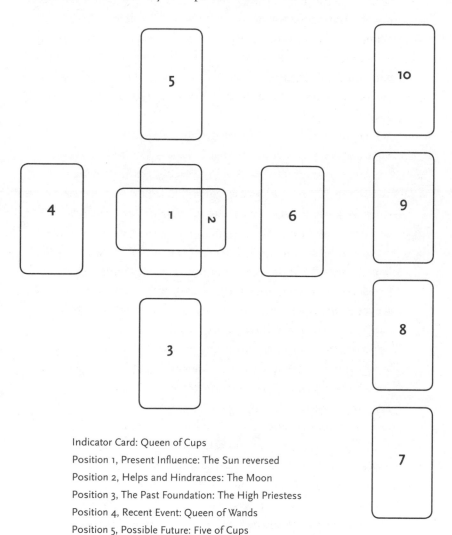

Indicator Card: Queen of Cups

Position 1, Present Influence: The Sun reversed

Position 2, Helps and Hindrances: The Moon

Position 3, The Past Foundation: The High Priestess

Position 4, Recent Event: Queen of Wands

Position 5, Possible Future: Five of Cups

Position 6, Immediate Future: Ace of Cups reversed

Position 7, Attitude: Five of Pentacles reversed

Position 8, Environment and Others: The Magician

Position 9, Hopes and Fears: Seven of Wands

Position 10, Final Outcome: The Hermit reversed

I began the reading with a focus on the Seeker, building up her strengths. This is a positive starting point that creates rapport, trust, and openness.

You are a caring woman who loves her mate. You both have similar values. You believe in love, marriage, relationship, and each other. Your relationship isn't happy currently and you are confused. When an issue arises, you become emotional. You are concerned about the ultimate failure of the relationship and are seeking hope for the marriage's survival and thriving.

The cards do point to hope for the future. You have courageously confronted your mate recently, looking for an airing of feelings. You've been focusing on accepting and loving yourself, gratefully counting your blessings. This has brought optimism that has opened your heart. When you are in this state, you feel a sense of destiny and a soul connection with your mate.

If you feel fearful or uncertain, your heart will close. There will be a challenge of your faith in love that will come in the near future. Remember to be positive. Faith allows the healing power of divine light and love to infuse your relationship with positive energy. Fear keeps you closed and unable to receive the help you desire.

There are powerful spiritual forces that want to see this relationship flourish. These forces will help you stay strong and centered, giving you courage and hope. The keys are within you and the choice is yours. Your willingness to be open to new methods of help is important. Old cycles of unhappiness won't repeat if you make healthy choices.

By nature you are a soulful person who is deeply rooted in the spiritual realm. You have found great solace and refuge in the love that the spirit has for you. The more time you spend in actively developing a relationship with your spiritual side, the happier you will be. This happiness will shift the relationship's energy in a real way. Your hope is that you will benefit by remaining brave as you assert your needs and desires.

You can continue to develop a thriving relationship with your spiritual side by any means you deem suitable. Yoga, prayer, meditation, reading inspirational books, writing in a journal, and exploring your dreams and daydreams are all ways to keep aligned with your spiritual side. These activities will reveal your soul's desires and gifts. The more you develop this inner relationship with your true soul power, the better you will feel about yourself. This will create the good feelings that will nurture your relationship.

You have a spiritual gift in need of expression. You can discover this by examining your childhood dreams and current desires. There may be a soulful activity that has always called to you, such as helping others, healing, teaching, creating something, or spiritual study. I advise following through with an aspiration, because it will open your heart and provide a lasting relationship with your soul. The personal strength derived from the fulfillment of an aspiration will provide increased self-esteem. This is what you will need in order to work on your marriage.

The solution to your question will involve coaching, counseling, or therapy in whatever manner you feel appropriate. The Hermit reversed often appears when the courage to seek guidance from others is being ignored. You cannot perform heart surgery on yourself, and this is a similar situation. You need the wisdom and know-how of an expert to help you and your marriage bloom. Your commitment to the process of self-awareness is crucial for your marriage's success. You cannot back out. You must trust the professionals, push through your fears, and seek and commit to counseling. If your mate doesn't want to attend at first, go alone. Trust in the process.

The cards suggest the following steps for attaining the secure love you are seeking. Stop doing what doesn't work, or hasn't worked in the past. Allow a wise counselor or therapist to help you. Focus on the positive. Seek fairness; treat yourself as you deserve to be treated. Develop your own relationship with your soul. No human relationship can give you what your soul yearns for. Regarding your marriage, don't throw the baby out with the bathwater.

Because positive, hopeful cards showed in this client's reading (Five of Pentacles reversed, Magician, Queen of Wands, Seven of Wands, and The High Priestess), I felt it was worthwhile to try some persuasion. I emphasized the areas (her mate's positive traits and her personal power and soul needs) on which it may be helpful for her to focus.

My alternative would have been simply to tell her she would never attain what she wanted with this union (Hermit reversed). The Hermit reversed can indicate a person who lacks knowledge. I felt that the client simply didn't know how to make her situation better. All she needed was a coach or teacher to give her the tools and know-how to improve her marriage.

The Magician and Queen of Wands represented hopeful resources for her to access. If more negative cards had appeared, I would have advised her to accept that this relationship wasn't viable for her.

To assess your progress in understanding the reading, reread my interpretation and write the name of the card you think I am interpreting in the space provided. You can check your answers at the end of this section.

1. You are a loving woman.

   _____

2. Your mate also shares these values.

   _____

3. You have courageously expressed your real needs and feelings recently.

   _____

4. When emotional issues arise, you become confused.

   _____

5. Currently, you are feeling this relationship is vulnerable and are unhappy about this.

    _____

6. You are concerned about it (the marriage) ultimately failing.

    _____

7. You are asking the cards for hope, because you want the union to survive and thrive.

    _____

8. Your cards do reveal hope for this relationship.

    _____

9. Recently, you've expressed your desires successfully.

    _____

10. This has opened your heart to accept the relationship with its imperfections, rather than focusing on its areas of lack and your needs.

    _____

11. Faith opens your heart and uncertainty closes it.

    _____

12. When you are in the flow, you have felt a sense of destiny about the relationship.

    _____

13. By focusing on your faith, spirituality, and blessings, you will have the keys to work through difficulties. Your

increased self-confidence will give you the courage to follow through on advice you will receive.

_____

14. You are by nature a soulful person, deeply rooted in the spiritual realm.

_____

15. Develop a consistent relationship with your spiritual side.

_____

16. Gift of the spirit.

_____

17. The solution is through coaching and therapy.

_____

18. Stop doing what hasn't worked.

_____

19. Focus on the positive aspects of yourself and your partner.

_____

20. Seek consistent soul development.

_____

21. Seek and commit to counseling.

_____

Answers:

1. The Queen of Cups represents a loving, nurturing, soulful woman.

2. You can often read the nature of the "other" person about whom the client is concerned by looking at the card occupying Position 8 of the Celtic Cross spread. The placement represents how others influence the question. In our example, the spouse appears as The Magician. The card is a good indication that he is devoted to the union and does bring many positive traits to their marriage.

3. The Queen of Wands in the placement of the Recent Event (Position 4) reveals she has courageously expressed herself in a positive way.

4. The Moon in Position 2—Hindrances.

5. The Sun reversed indicates a relationship that may fail, vulnerability, and a lack of know-how.

6. The Possible Future position is the Five of Cups, a good indication that she is concerned about the union dissolving.

7. The Five of Pentacles reversed is a return of hope and new faith in spiritual matters.

8. Although difficult to see at first glance, hope is evident in the reading. The High Priestess is the foundation (Position 3) of the relationship, indicating a soul connection between the couple. The Five of Pentacles reversed indicates spiritual regeneration. The Magician reveals her mate's sincere intention, while the Queen of Cups has faith in love. The Queen of Wands denotes the client's willingness to express herself courageously and her blossoming self-esteem. I felt the reversed Ace of Cups could easily be turned upright through more know-how, faith, and self-love. This was her personal

responsibility and challenge in the immediate future (Position 6, Immediate Future).

9. The Queen of Wands.

10. The Five of Pentacles reversed is now her attitude; she has hope.

11. The Ace of Cups blended with the Moon card.

12. High Priestess as the Foundation Card reveals her past experience and resources she can call upon.

13. Upright interpretation of the reversed Major Arcana. Cards that have a negative reversed meaning can simply indicate poor expression of the quality represented by the card. This is usually the case rather than a complete lack of the quality represented. Here is where the challenges of personal responsibility and self-improvement need to be emphasized. In this reading, there are no cards that indicate a malevolent energy, so I felt that the powers represented by the Major Arcana reversed were available to her if she chose empowerment. I focused on the positive and upright, rather than negative, interpretations of the reversed cards, as she was just coming into a realization of the powers represented by them. I knew this because of the courage and self-love displayed by the Queen of Wands in the recent past, and the renewed connection to her faith and soul, as seen in the Five of Pentacles reversed, the Queen of Cups, and The High Priestess.

14. High Priestess.

15. High Priestess.

16. High Priestess.

17. Positive interpretation of The Hermit reversed.

18. The Hermit reversed.

19. The High Priestess, Magician, Five of Pentacles reversed.

20. The High Priestess, upright Major Arcana, resolution of the Ace of Cups reversed.

21. Positive interpretation of The Hermit reversed.

Notice that I have used English here rather than "Tarot-speak." This simply means putting the card meanings in your own words and not emphasizing their titles. Metaphor is also a very powerful tool in a reading. In this example, I concluded the reading with this statement: "Don't throw the baby out with the bathwater."

CREATING A POSITIVE READING EXPERIENCE

A positive reading experience is defined as one where you feel a sense of rewarding revelation at its conclusion. As the reader, you feel satisfied that you've clearly discerned and communicated the cards' messages in a way that the recipient can easily and readily understand. You have done your job if the Seeker thanks you at the end of the session and offers comments like: "It was healing, useful, helpful, accurate, confirming or thought-provoking." Hopefully, you recorded the session for future reference.

The Unconscious in Tarot Reading

What motivates the Seeker to ask the Tarot for divination and guidance? That impulse or intuition comes from the unconscious—an influential force involved with the cards' messages. The Seeker's unconscious wants to communicate and, recognizing the Tarot as a vehicle, it seizes the opportunity to deliver its message through a reading.

Tarot cards serve as a connection between the wisdom of the Higher Self stored in the unconscious and the conscious mind. Like dreams, intuition, and synchronicity, they are a spiritual tool to help you understand your metaphysical journey. Tarot is an ideal vehicle for communication with your deeper subconscious and soul natures. This aspect of the psyche stores information about destiny, life lessons, karma, dharma, and the past, present, and future. It is important to consider this when formulating the questions that will guide your reading. After all, it is this power that has prompted the request for the reading.

The appropriate wording of the question asked of the Tarot is an important part of any reading. When I plan in advance for a session, I request that the Seeker really think about what he or she wants to learn from the cards. The unconscious hears the request and guides the process of selecting a question, theme, or focus for the sitting.

For example, the reading's question may be focused on one topic, yet the cards may describe a completely different issue. This phenomenon happens when the unconscious has information about an event unknown to the Seeker's conscious mind, or it has a message about a situation that has been placed on the back burner or repressed.

As a reader, you will often give information that the Seeker already knows, but needs to hear from an external source. This is empowering, because it is a validation of the Seeker's own assessment of the situation. He or she may respond with something like: "You haven't told me anything I don't already know, but it is really helpful to hear it from someone else." The way you explain the message may help them to frame or re-frame the situation. The reason that this characterizes a good reading is that the Seeker here demonstrates self-awareness rather than being dependent on you to provide answers.

For example, a woman came to me and said: "I feel as if I've been living outside of my real self. I want the cards to show me my true spiritual nature and how I can fulfill its purpose." She was in her early forties, and had brought a well thought-out question to the session. Her question for the Tarot was: "What does my true spiritual nature look like, and how can I fulfill its purpose on the earth plane?"

Here are examples of other types of questions you can ask the cards that prompt the unconscious to reveal its messages:

1. Please reveal the steps I can take to progress toward my goal of knowing and claiming my soul purpose or authentic self, health, relationship fulfillment, career, money, etc.

2. Show me what I need to understand about my current work situation, money, family, relationships, etc.

These types of questions will give you predictions and guidance to interpret. The Seeker's unconscious will reveal relevant history, spiritual lessons, and possibilities to consider. You can then discuss actions so that personal responsibility is included in the session. Our sample reading on page 19 has all of these components. The soul level is in good shape and has much to offer (High Priestess, Five of Pentacles reversed). The predictions of relationship challenges are clear. The guidance provided through the reading shows the Seeker how to act in accordance with her highest and best self.

The famous psychoanalyst Carl Jung believed in "the absolute knowledge of the unconscious." According to Jung, the unconscious knows the past, the present, and part of the future, and has a deep awareness regarding self and others. I believe that those who have a thinner veil between the conscious mind and this source of knowledge, or who have a closer kinship with it, are called intuitives and mystics.

One way to see the unconscious and its relationship with images and symbols that reveal the past, present, and future is to experiment with the following simple exercise. I call it the Life Story technique.

Lay the entire deck of cards face up on a table, and have someone unfamiliar with them, perhaps the Seeker, choose ten to fifteen cards and place them in random sequence from left to right. Then request that he or she tell the story of each card, reading from left to right. Without knowing the meaning of the cards, they will, uncannily, have placed the perception of his or her past, present, and future on the table. Using this technique, you can learn a great deal about your seeker's state of mind and unconscious beliefs as they describe where they have been and subconsciously believe they are headed. This exercise demonstrates how the subconscious recognizes the language of symbols and images, even if the person has no conscious knowledge of their meaning.

Imaginative Interaction

The unconscious uses the Tarot to impart wisdom. The following technique, which I call Imaginative Interaction, demonstrates the powerful connection between the cards and the wisdom aspect of the psyche. This is especially helpful when dealing with a challenging card or with a negative attitude from a Seeker about a positive card.

Sometimes during a reading, the Seeker is unable to see or accept the meaning of an important card in the layout. Take that card and place it in front of the client and ask him or her to describe what is occurring in the scene. What are the characters thinking and feeling and how are they behaving? Usually I say only: "Tell me what is going on in the card." I reassure clients that there is no right or wrong answer and that I am only interested in what they see.

As they speak, they reveal pure unconscious content—unedited and filled with meaning. Almost without fail, Seekers will describe

their own situation with precision, using their own words. This often leads to an "aha" moment in the reading that helps them integrate the cards' meanings. If they describe a card in a negative way, ask what the characters in the card can do to help the situation.

For example, Jim was confused about the career choices in his life. He was unhappy in his current job and was afraid of appearing incompetent. He felt inferior and was overwhelmed by responsibilities. His reading had the Eight of Swords in the eighth position of the Celtic card spread. This placement represents other people's influences and the environment surrounding the question. I felt this card was critical to an understanding of Jim's current situation. Sometimes, it is the so-called negative cards that give you the most information when "troubleshooting" in a session.

Jim described the Eight of Swords this way: "She is in a bad situation."

"What do you think she needs to do about it?" I asked

"She's got a blindfold on," he answered. "She needs to ask someone to help her take that off. Then she could see who to ask for help."

"So you think that you have a blindfold on regarding asking for help at work from the people around you?" I asked.

Jim thought for a moment and then said, "I never realized it before, but I don't think I have ever asked anyone for help at work. I thought I had to do everything for myself." Once he heard himself speak those words, Jim realized that he, indeed, was blindfolded and unable to see the support and access the assistance available to him at work.

An equally challenging situation occurs when someone cannot grasp the message of a positive card. Amy was seeking clarity in her life. She was a forty-eight-year-old professional in the midst of an unpleasant divorce and facing an uncertain future. She wanted the cards to show her what she needed to do to survive this stressful time in her life.

It was important to find a positive card to help her. Amy's reading had the Queen of Swords in the third house of the Zodiac spread. This house, or sector of the zodiac wheel, represents the conscious mind and often reveals a client's general outlook on life.

I placed the Queen of Swords directly in front of Amy and asked her for a character description of the card.

"She seems very determined and focused on her sword," Amy replied.

"What does the sword mean to you?" I asked.

"Power, strength, defense. Something used to cut through obstacles," she answered.

"How did the Queen become strong and powerful?" I asked.

"By using mind over matter," Amy said. "She stayed sharp; she focused on her goal. She knew what was right, and she was determined to accomplish it."

I asked Amy if she saw how her answer related to her attitude and thinking concerning her divorce.

She said, "I've always been an independent person and had my own ideas. I know I am smart and capable, and I'm determined to get through this. I just have to keep focused on my strengths instead of my weaknesses."

In both examples, a precise, helpful, and clear message came through from the unconscious by interacting with the cards. This sense of empowerment is enhanced by hearing the message of the cards spoken aloud and in the client's own words.

The Life Story and Imaginative Interaction techniques provide tools for the reader to go beyond the standard Tarot interpretation. The methods work very well because the unconscious employs the most meaningful ways to get its message across using the Seeker's own words, provoking memory and initiating relevant and often problem-solving guidance. Your role as a reader is to facilitate this process gently by asking questions and validating your clients' responses. Continue to interact until they arrive at a resolution or revelation, as shown in our examples.

DESIGNING EFFECTIVE QUESTIONS

Seekers often have difficulty defining what they truly want to get out of a reading. It is important that they have a clear intention in mind before they begin to shuffle the cards. To assist them, I say the following:

I want to help you get the most out of the sitting. You know better than I do what you want to explore. I want to help you design your reading question around what you really want to know.

Usually, at this point, clients volunteer a lot of information. Spend a few minutes helping them formulate a clear definition of what they want the cards to reveal. Refer to the suggestions on page 29 for examples. A simple request for clarity concerning a topic is always effective. Asking for truth, guidance, or information about how the future looks about a topic is certain to create a helpful card consultation. An attitude of "How can I best serve you?" also sets the stage for a meaningful Tarot sitting.

If a timeline is important, incorporate it into the question—for example: "Show me my work situation for the next six months." Or "Show me how my school term will end in June." Or "What does my love life look like for the coming year?" Since the cards contain messages relayed through imagery, asking for information about the future or guidance that includes how a situation will develop gives a visual reference that may be relevant for the Seeker. You might say:

We are looking at a road map of where you are in the here and now, and future possibilities. The reading will reveal potentials for the future, and choices will be presented to you. This reading will give you guidance, predictions, and knowledge. What you do with this information is up to you."

BONDING WITH THE SEEKER

Creating a bond of trust with the Seeker should happen as soon as possible during a session. The way to build trust is to be calm, open, and self-assured. Don't be unfocused or self-absorbed. Center all your energy on the reading. There should be very little small talk. Excess chatting will lower the vibration in the session, possibly blocking the psychic information offered by the cards.

You can use a preamble to create warmth and rapport during the initial conversation. Describe your history with the Tarot, your perception of how the cards operate, your special interpretive style, and the particular intuitive gifts you bring to the sitting. Explain the amount of time your typical reading lasts and then ask if the client has any questions. Answer the inquiries as honestly as possible; offer a fair and balanced perspective.

Another way to dialogue with Seekers is to inquire about their prior experience with readers. This will reveal their familiarity, expectations, and reservations. These can then be discussed beforehand, thereby allaying concerns. This facilitates a clearer path through which the unconscious can communicate the message of the cards during the sitting.

Before you begin the reading, inform the Seeker that you will be checking periodically to ensure that your interpretation makes sense. Your client may not agree with it, but you do need to make sure that you are "on the same page."

This checking can sometimes be perceived by clients as an invitation to reveal too much information by telling you more than you need to hear. This may turn the reading into a therapy session, rather than a consultation. When this happens, you can say:

I only need confirmation from you; if you go into a conversation with me, you will be preventing the flow of the reading.

Usually, this is enough to get the reading back on track.

After the initial topic for the session has been discussed, the question formulated, and the cards dealt, the Seeker may continue to talk! You can say to him or her:

I really want you to get the most out of this reading, so at this point we need to focus on what the cards are saying about your question. I need to devote all my attention to the messages I am receiving and interpreting for you.

If the Seeker still continues to speak or lapses back into a dialogue, close your eyes. The chatter will stop, and you then can thank the client for assuming a receptive role so the messages that will benefit can be delivered successfully.

Seekers who ultimately insist on talking during the session are either afraid or resistant to hearing the card's insights, or their processing style may simply involve speaking aloud to facilitate understanding. Sometimes Seekers simply want a sounding board and someone to listen to and agree with their opinions. This is unfortunate, and all you can do is say what you see, then listen and be thankful that you've explained that the session has a specific time limitation! It is possible that, through their downloading of information, they will realize something of importance. Do not judge the session; simply ask that truth, in whatever form it comes, be revealed to the good of all and harm of none.

HANDLING A NEGATIVE READING

One challenge that is inevitable when reading the Tarot is knowing how to handle a negative card or layout. Here are some tips for extracting a helpful message from an unpleasant spread.

Find a positive card or cards in the spread. Have the Seeker describe what he or she sees in those cards as far as constructive imagery goes, including characters' personality traits or other features. This can trigger personal insights about a client's situation, and the interaction may lessen the effects of, or give possible solutions to, the original negative message. You can also use the upright meanings of an important card for help, as I did with the reversed Hermit card in our sample reading on page 21. Another option is to have the client choose a helping card randomly from the deck and use its meaning for guidance.

Honesty is ultimately appreciated. But you will feel more confident delivering bad news if you develop a few key phrases ahead of time. Some examples are: "This isn't to your advantage." Or "This

situation doesn't serve your highest and best good." Other gentle
and effective comments about unfavorable forecasts are, "The cards
are suggesting disappointment," or "The cards are suggesting unfavorable circumstances,"or "I don't think this will bring happiness
for you."

ASSESSING THE CENTRAL MESSAGE
OF A READING

Make an overall assessment of a layout before you interpret specific cards to provide a focus and central theme you can emphasize during your reading. Begin your observations by finding the
Major Arcana. These cards represent the lessons and spiritual
powers you explain during the sitting. They provide the themes or
ultimate message of the reading. If the cards are upright, emphasize the virtues and powers; if they are reversed, use the upright
meaning as guidance by explaining the favorable attributes and
suggesting they be applied to the situation.

Next, find the dominant suit elements. Upright and positive cards represent favorable traits. For example, if many positive
upright Wands appear, fortitude, courage, and dedication are the
strengths indicated.

If a suit is dominant but unfavorable—for example, if there
are either negative reversals or cards appearing with negative upright
cards—the situation requires correction. For example, clients with
many negative upright Sword cards appearing may experience an
injustice. They may not be treating themselves fairly, or may be the
victims of external injustice. By utilizing the upright meaning of
the Swords—i.e., doing oneself justice, using clear thinking, and
acting based on self-esteem—you can suggest guidance that will
improve the situation.

Next, find the Court cards. Utilize your three favorite meanings
for each suit from Chapter I to describe the character qualities of
the Seeker and/or the people involved with the question. Finally,
focus on the Minor Arcana, which describe the client's actual sce-

nario or situation—in other words, how the circumstance is occurring in the real world.

THEMES FOR THE COURT CARDS

Each Court card has its own theme. Use these suggestions to guide your interpretation.

Wands: Outgoing, adventurous, strong feelings of appropriateness or inappropriateness; know how they feel; personable, ambitious, noble; emanates self-esteem; strong likes and dislikes. Asks: "How does the topic relate to myself and others? How do I feel about this or that?"

Cups: Introverted, imaginative, needs to feel loved; emotionally connected, intuitive, nurturing, values creativity and the giving and receiving of love; emanates compassion; interested in future possibilities. Asks: "What does the topic mean?"

Swords: Inquisitive, bright; good oral and written skills, communicative; loves knowledge and information; seeks variety; likes precision. Asks: "What is the explanation of the topic?"

Pentacles: Security-conscious, capable, pragmatic; prosperous, sensuous, tactile; detail-oriented, factual; nature loving. Asks: "What is the definition of the subject?"

USING THE CARDS FOR DECISION-MAKING

People who want help making a decision often turn to the Tarot for guidance. Seekers should not, however, ask the cards, "Will I make the correct choice?" Instead, perform two separate Celtic Cross or other card spreads and ask: "What will the outcome look like if I take path A? What does the future look like if I choose path B?"

If the Lovers card appears in one of the readings, the Seeker is making the correct decision. The Ace of Swords and upright Aces in general, as well as upright Court cards, indicate a beneficial direction. All upright Major Arcana, with the exception of The Devil, The Tower, and The Moon, indicate good choice-making.

THE NEGATIVE SEEKER

Inevitably, you'll encounter the situation where someone wants a reading, then appears to doubt your ability or behaves in a negative way. Approach the sitting with respect, and your Seeker will respond accordingly. The issues that motivate your sessions are your clients' not yours. It is *their* fears, prior unpleasant experiences, skepticism, and negativity that may cause them to doubt you.

Sometimes, there may be bad chemistry between a reader and a Seeker. When this happens, it is best to end the session, because you cannot tune in on the person or their question. It is very important that you not leave the Seeker thinking that something terrible or too awful to forecast is the reason you are terminating the session. Explain that a poor connection and your inability to tune in can happen sometimes and that it is best, in your experience, to end the session. Honesty is always best and will be appreciated.

One way to create a rapport and alleviate negativity is to begin the session by introducing yourself. Tell the Seeker who you are and your background in Tarot reading. Explain why you read the cards and how you perceive their messages as guidance and helpful forecasts for the benefit of others, as well as for yourself. Indicate how long you have been a reader. If you are just beginning reading for others, share this fact and then speak about the amount of time you've spent studying the cards.

Discuss other intuitive talents that you may bring to the session. For example, you may be channeling or reading auras or including an interpretation of a client's astrological chart. It is important that you make sure your clients are aware if you're using a variety of techniques. Sometimes they may have an aversion to a particular interpretive method, and it is important that you know that before you begin, so you can adapt your reading accordingly.

THE UNFORESEEN FUTURE

Tarot cards provide insight, direction, and prediction. They offer confirmation, clarity, and truth, especially if you ask for these qualities as you concentrate on a question and shuffle the cards. The cards interact with the unconscious mind, with soul knowledge, and with past, present, and future destiny. Some of this data is mutable or variable, subject to change from your will's influence and fluctuating life situations. Other information is destined and immutable.

A Tarot reading provides guidance from the soul's wisdom. Your soul is vast and not controlled by your ego and will. It has a timing and intention different from the ego's and is much more adept in knowing the true timing of future events. It will not reveal what you are not ready to receive. Predictions that seem as if they "should" have been revealed according to your ego may remain hidden, while other unexpected events may be clearly indicated. Since the cards' source is the soul, you can trust that you may say what is presented in the spread with a clear conscience.

There are numerous reasons why the cards are not always correct. Options, opportunities, and advice may be ignored. Sometimes, future changes are simply unforeseen. Not all events are predetermined; our lives are a combination of free will and destiny. Perhaps the conscious mind could not handle certain information if it were revealed. Or perhaps nothing can be done regarding a circumstance. Destiny may be in control, and the subconscious protects us from too much awareness of things that can not be altered. I also feel that, sometimes, the future does not unfold the way it was predicted because another karmic element supersedes the one described by the cards. In every prognostic, forecasting, and diagnostic technique, there are some inaccuracies; the predictive aspect of card reading is no different.

COMMUNICATING PREDICTIONS

Athough most Seekers expect that their readings will include predictions, insisting that your divination is guaranteed to happen is unrealistic. Sometimes Seekers will pressure you to promise or guarantee your forecast; this is not practical. You can handle this request by stating that you are accurate 80 to 90 percent of the time. Describe the future as you see it with confidence, but refrain from communicating an absolute certainty.

It is kinder to use phrasing that allows more personal empowerment when forecasting negative circumstances, outcomes, or events. Therefore, temper your predictive phrases. Wording such as "you will fail," "you will be harmed," or other negative forecasts of gloom and doom are not helpful. Instead, choose words like "may occur," "could happen," or "this is what the cards seem to be saying."

For example, when commenting on a negative future, say something like, "The cards are indicating an unfulfilling trend." Or "You may not be pleased with how things turn out." This is still predictive, but gentle rather than dramatic, yet the message is still clear. You can then go on to describe the specific card's meaning.

Predicting time sequences is easier said than done. People are unrealistic and anxious when difficulties arise, wanting them immediately resolved without any pain. It is human nature to become impatient regarding that which is near and dear. Don't be pressured by your clients' demands for a time frame. If you are talking about months and not weeks, tell them that, whether it pleases them or not.

Here, we'll look at effective communication techniques that help you interpret the cards' messages successfully.

The Analogy Style

I often encounter readings filled with possibilities that the client doesn't realize. Use this technique when you are reading for an individual who is attached to an unproductive desire that will not be fulfilled or is unable to see other possibilities.

The analogy I use is that of a smorgasbord. I tell the client to imagine being at an elaborate buffet filled with many delicious foods, then choosing to eat only the celery sticks, without seeing all the more wonderful choices available. The client, by returning for more celery sticks, is staying with the familiar, safe life choice, even though it is not very nourishing—remaining in a comfort zone even if it is a miserable one!

Another dilemma often brought to the cards is an unfulfilled love wish or unrequited love, in which a person's reading may indicate that a desire will not be fulfilled, but he or she may be unable to perceive this reality. Here is a real-life situation that illustrates my point.

I wanted to help a client progress in her life. I knew because of her repetitive visits to me that she was stuck waiting for a married man to leave his wife. The cards revealed ultimate disappointment for the relationship. During the reading, I used an analogy. I picked up my coffee cup, held it as I would a telephone, and pretended to order a pizza. I then turned to the client and said:

This is what you are trying to do. You are trying to order a pizza from a coffee cup, and it is never going to happen. It is perfectly fine and appropriate to want the pizza, but you have to get it from the suitable source.

I wanted to help the client see that her desire for love was correct, but that she needed to move on to find it with a fitting partner.

Analogies can be very helpful; they make the card's message lucid and down-to-earth. They allow you to place the reading's message in a context that the Seeker can understand. This is very memorable and empowering for both the Seeker and you.

HANDLING A
DISCOURAGING FORECAST

In situations where the Seeker needs a balanced perspective to cope with a discouraging message, I suggest another reading cast about a positive future possibility. For example, a marriage is dissolving, and there is no hope for reconciliation. Rather than leaving the Seeker sad and despondent, ask permission to look into the future, post-divorce, to see who will arrive bringing new hope and happiness.

Cast a second spread with this question in mind. It is very helpful to give a positive indication that current problems will be conquered and to show the light at the end of the tunnel. This message will often be a source of hope when life seems bleak.

PREPARING FOR A READING

Most practiced readers prepare both psychically and emotionally for their readings. Breathe deeply and center yourself using prayer or affirmation. Then call upon the forces of light and surround yourself with the white light of protection. Affirm that you are an agent for the power of good. You may want to hold a crystal or stone of your choice. A double-pointed quartz crystal, which acts as a wand or dual current, is my favorite. Amethyst wands are strong psychically, as are numerous other blue, violet, or clear crystals and stones.

Shuffle the deck before the Seeker shuffles, asking for protection, truth, and guidance, and to be a clear channel for communication from the cards. Imagine white light pouring from your hands, heart, and crown chakra into the deck, activating the potency of the Tarot. If you have a favorite incense, burn it along with a candle.

The spiritual icon associated with the Tarot is the falcon or hawk, mysteriously pictured in the Albano-Waite deck in the Nine of Pentacles. This bird relates to the Egyptian god Horus, who presides over the cards. His power is solar and appears within a golden light.

The Tarot's guardian angel is Heru, or HRU, from the name Heru-ra-ha, the sacred name of the Egyptian child-god, Horus. "Heru" is the traditional invocation used to clear your deck before performing a reading. You can also use it to consecrate the deck when it is first used.

The angel associated with the Tarot is the Archangel Uriel, who corresponds to The Hermit. Uriel represents the secret ancient wisdom and oracular knowledge. You can visualize him or the High Priestess standing behind you and guiding the reading.

Receiving Psychic Information

Your innate psychic gift will be activated when you perform readings. Psychic ability can be experienced through various senses. Sometimes it is a "feeling" in the gut. Or it may be a thought that enters your mind that seems incongruous with your personal experience.

One of the hallmarks of a psychic prompting is having an unshakable "knowing" about a person or situation, even when no factual evidence exists to confirm the information. This "knowing" often occurs at the start of a reading, then persistently repeats itself during the sitting. When you share the message with your client, you find that the information is accurate.

Clairvoyance (literally "clear seeing") is the perception of images, information, symbols, and/or colors inside your mind's eye. These pictures may also appear around a person in his or her auric field, or as a spirit entity, guide, teacher, or healer standing beside or behind the Seeker.

Clairvoyants may experience profound psychic impact from the symbols of the Tarot. The images on the cards provide a plethora of visual information. They were designed to invite meditation on their imagery and to tell a story while teaching important arcane lessons.

You may find that some of the images from a card become filled with life and draw your attention. If this occurs, touch the card, quiet yourself, and become open and receptive. You will receive the message of the card through your intuition and inner vision.

Clairaudience (literally "clear hearing") can occur on its own or in conjunction with other psychic faculties. It is a direct hearing of information from an outside source and feels as if you are listening to your own thoughts. This sense functions from the intuition and provides guidance about future and present circumstances. If the content of the message has no relevance to you, it may be revealing significant information about the Seeker. Simply say what you hear and ask for confirmation or a reason why this message is being transmitted. Once you and the Seeker understand the initial message, more information may be channeled to you.

Clairsentience (literally "clear sensing or feeling") occurs when you experience bodily sensations—a feeling in your gut, a touch, warmth or a chill, pulsing or tingling in a specific location in your body like your palms or the top and back of your head, or heat or cold in your spinal column. Occasionally, smells also convey psychic communication. When this happens, sensation is the medium, and you need to ask your intuition what the feeling or scent is meant to convey.

The challenge for those who are clairsentient is to translate these feelings into useful information. Begin to form a vocabulary of these feelings by keeping a journal of your sensing and your personal associations. For example, a certain scent may represent a certain circumstance to you. Or a twitch in a certain place may indicate you are correct in your assessment. Or feelings of stagnation or expansiveness may be relevant in the context of a reading's past, present, or future.

Intuitive vision and hearing may accompany clairsentience. Readers who have these skills may instinctively touch the cards as they read for a client. Like clairvoyants, they also respond strongly to color. As you observe a layout, you may be struck by a color or a series of colors that stand out. You can glean further information by simply getting a feel for what the color seems to convey.

Clairsentience is often found in those who possess the gift of healing. Healers sense and "feel" energies within and around the body. Earth-sign individuals (Taurus, Virgo, and Capricorn), or those with strong earth signs in their chart may possess this gift.

Clairsentients can develop healing and psychic abilities through yoga, Tai Chi, sacred dance, and spiritual breathing techniques. These activities are important for all intuitives, because they often are "ungrounded," living in their heads and disconnected from their bodies, which can lead to poor health habits and underdeveloped practical life skills.

All these psychic aptitudes may be experienced and developed through the Tarot, although they exist independently of it. The presence of all these intuitive gifts is called polysentience.

Notice your bodily sensations when performing readings. You may experience energy shifts that correspond to the messages in the layout. Look at the cards in the spread. Notice their gestures and feel what the characters are doing to deepen your interpretation.

Energy changes of a positive nature—like a feeling of expansiveness, sacredness, warmth, solace, and love—also occur because the Higher Self, teacher/healer, or guardian draws close to bring information during the reading. Your spirit guide or the client's guide may be present during a session. The Hermit meditation on page 172 offers the experiences of connecting to your guides and teachers.

Here is an example of how clairaudience occurs during a sitting. While a client was shuffling and focusing on her question, I heard a voice say to me, "Talk to her about the cancer." I was concerned about mentioning this subject. The message came back to me that it was not she, but someone in her family, with cancer and I was to talk to her about it.

I laid out the cut and found the Three of Wands reversed in the past, Judgement reversed in the present, and the Seven of Pentacles reversed in the future. At this point, I felt I had to relay the information. I gently asked if there was a problem around her having to do with cancer. She confirmed that her sister had just had a cancer operation that week. The cards in the cut provided more information about the matter that I had not perceived clairaudiently.

Judgement reversed indicated that the sister was not perfectly cured, because its reversed meaning implies lack of release about the matter. The Three of Wands reversed in the past can represent growth in the wrong direction or growth of a negative nature. It suggested to me the growth of the cancer in three locations. The Seven of Pentacles reversed in the future indicated that there might be more medical problems to come. Something about the immune system or further internal decline and deterioration would require attention. The best practice is to learn to trust any clairaudient information received, take the leap of faith, and communicate its message.

Another example involved impressions I received both clairvoyantly and clairsentiently. I had many visual impressions appearing rapidly in my mind's eye while a client was shuffling the cards. I saw, of all things, the *Titanic*. At the same moment, a "knowing" came over me about the client's husband working as a storywriter. I inquired by simply presenting the information as I was shown, not attempting to interpret, just relaying the images.

Message confirmation came as she revealed that her husband had written and subsequently published a book about *Titanic* and was looking forward to a reprinting after a sellout run. I incorporated the clairvoyant message into the Tarot spread using the Zodiac layout and checked the spouse's finances. Position 8, which governs the partner's resources, held a positive card, the Wheel of Fortune. I determined that he would be receiving substantial income increases involving the book.

Often, during a reading, a client will not immediately understand a message or meaning. This is very common. Do not change your perception. Leave it with the client and move on. Chances are that, by the end of the session, the information will be understood.

For example, an inexperienced reader saw The Hierophant in the past cut pile of an individual she was advising. She was moved to say that the Seeker had experienced a rigid, conventional person in her past in connection with the query, which was a relationship-romance question.

"No," she replied "Mr. X is not like that at all." The reader did not modify or change her opinion.

"Was your father like that in the past?" the reader asked.

"No," was the reply. Then, all of a sudden, a lightbulb went on for the woman. Indeed, her prior boyfriend had had those characteristics and was influencing her feelings about her current relationship in a way she had not realized. This is the "aha!" you are looking for, and it was very helpful in guiding the remainder of the reading's interpretation, as well as validating the reader's abilities.

RECOGNIZING CHANNELED INFORMATION

During a reading, pay attention to the vocabulary and images you use. If you are using words or examples that are not in your own experience, you may be channeling information from the Seeker's subconscious and/or Higher Self. It may serve you to ask if the information describes something in his or her history. Perhaps a spirit relative is present and guiding the flow of communication.

Your mode of perception will open and accelerate as you per-form more readings. This is one of the reasons to seek out the experience of divining for other people. When you receive chan-neled information, give it promptly just as you receive it. Do not attempt to interpret the symbols or images at first. Simply say what you have received exactly the way it was given, and then ask for feedback.

The feedback may require a bit of conversation. If you feel that the Seeker is open to making a statement regarding your impres-sions, ask for a comment. While your client is speaking, more information may come forward in your mind's eye, your hearing, or as a simple "knowing." Give the new information. If the client is defensive or otherwise closed, simply state the message, say that you will leave it with the person so that he or she can remember it was mentioned. Then move on.

If the information makes no sense to the Seeker, ask yourself what the images mean to you. Within a few minutes, a "knowing" will enter your mind, consisting of an association between your personal history or own experience and the imagery.

For example, Diane paused during a sitting with Marta, a Seeker previously unknown to her. She felt energy coming from one of the cards, the Ace of Cups. Her immediate reaction was to touch that card. An image of a house floating in the air appeared in her mind. Suddenly, the roof flew off and the house inverted! "What shall I say about this?" she mused. Diane described the scene to Marta, who was unimpressed.

Then Diane asked silently for guidance about the meaning of the vision. Her deceased grandfather's voice rang in her ears saying, "Penny wise, pound foolish." She then asked Marta what that phrase meant to her. "Oh, my grandfather used to say that to me when he gave me my birthday card. It was always a money envelope."

Now Diane had what she needed. "Could your question have an element of 'Penny wise, pound foolish' to it?" she asked. "In other words, paying too much attention to the small things and not looking at the big picture?"

Marta carefully pondered the question. "Yes," she said. "I have been so focused on details at work that I missed an application deadline for a job I wanted that would have meant a promotion with increased pay."

"I sense your grandfather is offering this guidance to you through the cards," said Diane.

"I think you're right," said Marta. "Today is my birthday."

Diane wondered if the Seeker's grandfather was present for the session, since relatives who have passed on often appear as guides. She then saw the first image of the house, upright, with the roof restored. This confirmed the grandfather's presence and subsequent relief that the house had been put right. The grandfather had visited from the spirit world and was content with the outcome of Diane's passage of the message to Marta.

Typically, these "visits" don't last long, which is why, as a reader, you must give the information in a timely fashion. Trust that the information is meant to be given, because you have prayed and meditated, asking that only knowledge that serves the higher good for the Seeker be revealed.

You now have new skills for interpreting the cards, whether consulting them for others or yourself. Chapter 3 features some of the experiences that come with being a Tarot reader. It also includes fun, innovative ways to interact with the cards.

· 3 ·

BEST READING PRACTICES

This chapter focuses on the real-life experiences of Tarot readers. I share my strategies for maintaining your integrity and dignity when handling a variety of social situations you'll encounter as a Tarot person. We explore topics central to the reader's experience, like the value of reading for others and protection from psychic intrusion.

Understanding how the Tarot operates through study and the analysis of layouts is the usual course a Tarot student takes. I believe my fun, classic, and nontraditional ways of learning the cards are educational and innovative. They will spark your creative imagination. Most people learn by enjoying interactive activities, so I close this chapter with experiential Tarot practices that are sure to increase your understanding of the cards.

SOCIAL DILEMMAS FOR READERS

Awkward social situations are inevitable when you become known as a Tarot reader. These scenarios are less tricky when you're prepared for them in advance. The strategies and principles in this section will help you manage these predicaments with assuredness and dignity.

Beware of being befriended by people who solicit your companionship because they perceive you as validating them and their future aspirations. This dilemma crops up when someone is unable or unwilling to separate your favorable reading for them from you as an individual. Some individuals will invite you into their circle out of a superstitious belief that, somehow, if you believe in them, their dreams will come true. Your presence has the imbued quality of a talisman or a good-luck charm.

Others may regard you as a source to confide in and "dump" on or as an all-seeing problem-solver. This blurs the line of friendship and leaves you giving, without receiving much in return.

If you suspect a friendship has these attitudes at its foundation, I advise you to test the waters. Don't be a convenient, psychic, all-seeing ally, a confidant, or an on-call problem-solver. Instead, just behave as you naturally would toward a friend and treat the person as you do your other companions. If the friendship evaporates, it wasn't true to begin with.

I had a "friend" who invited me to lunch, then pulled out her Tarot deck from her purse and proceeded to shuffle the cards. She asked repeated questions, laid out the readings in front of me on the restaurant table, and asked me to "just look at this for a moment."

Much to my chagrin, I complied. But I resolved to respond politely but firmly if I were put on the spot in the future. The next time she pulled out her Tarot deck at a restaurant table, I explained that I felt uncomfortable performing readings in that setting. I then told her I had another engagement and departed.

Another friend invited me to a dinner party he was hosting; I was skeptical about the intention of his invitation. I specifically asked if I would encounter guests of the "oh you can see the future, tell me mine" type. He assured me there was no need for concern.

One of the guests sought me out as soon as he arrived. He stuck his palms in my face and said, "I hear you can read palms. What do you see for me?" Fortunately for me, I don't read palms! In hindsight, I realize my host was very motivated by his need to impress people and was status-oriented in his companionship choices.

I have learned to handle those social situations in which you are accosted by guests who want a free reading or treat you as if you are always open to psychic messages. I simply say: "I don't perform readings outside of my office, and I only 'tune in to' my psychic ability during a client's session. Here is my business card if you'd like to call for an appointment." I have taught my companions to watch for situations like this and to yank me away from people who hurl everything from insults to bouquets in my direction.

If you do want this type of attention, have someone else speak about your excellent reading skills on your behalf. I advise against becoming a sideshow at a party. It can signal a sense of self-importance and attention-seeking that does not serve the integrity and dignity that serious Tarot practice deserves.

The general public regards the Tarot with a mixture of glamour, hype, curiosity, amazement, and ridicule. It is your responsibility to treat the cards with the respect they deserve and not to trivialize your craft. If you want to mix your social and Tarot worlds, have a reading party where card consultation is the evening's theme.

HANDLING CHALLENGING SEEKERS

The "prove-it-to-me" scenario occurs when an individual approaches a reading expecting you to provide immediate impressive psychic information about his or her life. Often, this type of client has decided in advance what you should reveal in order to be believed. Remember that the reading is not about proving how psychic you are according to your seeker's preconceived notions.

The best practice is to explain the nature of a reading as a blend of prediction and guidance derived from your client's own Higher Self. The content of the reading will reveal what he or she needs to hear at this time. The messages will be translated by you, using the Tarot cards, and will comment on expected and unexpected subjects.

The Needy

Tarot divination can attract needy people who want you to solve their problems for them. These needy types will sometimes bully you or act as victims, pressuring you to tell them what to do and how to live their lives. Often, they will attempt to intimidate you into divining their future according to their preconceived notions. They are after wish fulfillment without having to act or modify their behavior. These individuals may be open to hearing only what they want to hear. Presumably, you are their last resort— possibly in their eleventh hour—and they want you to wave a magic wand to make everything better.

For these clients, it is important to emphasize personal responsibility. Only they can alter their own reactions and themselves. Nor can they change other people. This may cause some hostility, because you are telling them something they don't want to hear. Needy folks are in an emotional state. They seek solutions without facing their own contributions to the problem. As a reader, the danger is that you can be drawn into those emotions and resort to telling them what they want to hear through the pressure created by their desperation. You don't want to disappoint them. If you concede to their needs, they may leave the session happy and relieved, but your reading may be inaccurate and ultimately disappointing (not to mention possibly psychologically damaging or dangerous!).

Keep the reading focused on their questions and maintain a balance between the personal responsibility you see and the predictive information the cards reveal. Do not prolong the reading; trust that your words will resonate when their souls can hear them. Remember to focus on the positive and what they have going for them, especially their character strengths.

The Greedy

Greedy clients try to extend the allotted time for the session. They may ask, "What else do you see?" hoping to prolong the sitting by probing for specifics and more detailed information—to the point of exhausting both you and the subject.

For these clients, always begin your sitting by explaining how long the reading will take and that you will allow time for their questions. For example, "The reading, including your questions, will take approximately an hour, and we may go over ten to fifteen minutes. If you want more time, we can arrange another session. How does that sound to you?" Most likely, they will agree and you will have succeeded in establishing a time boundary for both of you.

The Manipulators

Manipulation can take place when Seekers want you to give another person "a good talking to" on their behalf. This situation arises when you have accurately described the behavior or attitude of someone in their lives. They then request that you read for that person and tell them the information that came to light during the session. When someone attempts to make you do this, just explain that it is not your job to speak on anyone's behalf.

I developed the habit of asking my clients, not only what brings them for a reading, but also who sent them. If the referral connects with someone who made this request known during a prior session and I sense coercion, I may ask, "Do you really want this reading, or have you been coerced into coming?" Often, the new Seeker will admit to having been pressured into the consultation. Even so, this desire for a reading may be legitimate.

I simply state that the cards will reveal what is meant to be known and focus completely on the current reading, while erasing the prior one from my mind.

The Superstitious

These sessions usually begin with clients anxiously requesting, "Tell me everything you see, don't hold back." This is usually an indicator that they are hoping to hear that someone has put a hex on them or that evil enemies are working against them. They may be desirous of a prediction that someone they dislike is going to pass away. I ignore all these subjects. At the end of the reading, they will inevitably ask about one or all of them. I just say that I didn't see anything of that nature in the reading. When you are asked to align your Tarot interpretations with negativity, you have the right to decline.

The Hostile

Watch for defensive posturing (arms crossed, pushing away from the table, turning sideways, or an inability to look you in the eye). These people have secrets. They feel vulnerable. They may be afraid or be lying to others, to themselves, or to you. Often, their behavior is hostile because they feel secretly threatened by having a reading. They may be worried about what the cards will reveal and what you may discover about them.

As a reader, ask yourself how you will feel if you get hostile reactions from people. You may be unmoved by these responses. If you have difficulty with them, however, you need to develop a coping strategy—like continuing to read what the cards reveal and ignoring the attitude of hostility.

Usually, these situations become apparent as soon as the reading begins. When you ask for confirmation, you may get an ambivalent reply like, "That's true for everyone, isn't it?" or "Well, I guess so," or "I suppose so," or "Sort of." Ask if the client would like you to be more specific. Go into more detail about the cards you have already interpreted. Then ask, "Does this relate to your inquiry or make sense to you?"

If the resistance continues—"I'd rather not say," or "Just go ahead and tell me what you see"—explain that you need to know that the information you are giving makes sense and relates to the question. Your interpretation may be precise, but the message may require different wording. Try rephrasing what you have said. If hostile clients still remain closed and resistant, you can say, "Well, I am just going to go ahead and tell you what I see then." It may be just a matter of a few more minutes before they confirm that you are making sense, and you can continue with a better level of trust. It is rare for hostility to last for the whole session.

Don't take these clients' hostile retorts personally. Say what you see and ask politely if any questions remain unanswered at the end of the reading. If they offer a question, comment on it; if not, thank them for their time. Most of all, understand that their misgivings are not your problem.

Take a break afterward rather than immediately performing another reading. Clear your energy field with a smudge stick or incense. Drink pure water and say a prayer or affirmation, surround yourself with white light, and ask that any and all negativity be removed from you, your energy field, your cards, and the environment.

The Unresolved

People can become obsessed with a topic, repeatedly asking the same question of the cards. This is usually prompted by unresolved problems or unfulfilled wishes. These readings are always fraught with complications, and the client may require a counselor, coach, advisor, or healer, not a Tarot reader. Provide encouragement that things will be alright, but always direct the personal responsibility back to the Seeker.

Clients who continually ask the same question are always characterized by behaviors that support "staying stuck." Their conscious wish is to stop suffering, so they seek your advice in a reading. But they never take any action because they are too fearful.

You may find yourself actually telling them what to do, but they refuse to act. The reading becomes a release valve. By asking the cards about the problem, these clients feel a sense of relief, but still neglect to face the problem and do anything about it.

For these clients, suggest a separate reading geared toward what the cards reveal about how their future might be if they took action. You may also encourage them to ask the cards to describe the outcome of engaging a therapist or coach, or some other problem-solving strategy. The key is to help them admit that they are stuck and need encouragement to act. This positive, proactive approach supports their desire to evolve and helps place the responsibility back on their shoulders.

The Spy

Seekers who request information about their spouses, ex-spouses, lovers, family members, coworkers, bosses, or enemies I call "spies." Their queries may focus on what these associates are really doing, or how they really feel about the client. Spies often request readings because they are separated from the subject of their inquiry.

Usually, these clients desire reassurance concerning their beliefs about the other individuals, but often the desire is just to pry into another person's life. If this feels out of the bounds of your integrity or if you feel as if you are spying, you can refuse to read about the other person and, instead, offer a reading about how the individual will influence the Seeker's life. This can reveal an ethical version of both how the other person feels and what they will bring to the life of your client.

STYLES OF CARD SPREADS

Choosing the appropriate style of spread for a Seeker's specific needs is essential for a successful session. The best practice is to become familiar with a variety of card spreads designed for diverse inquiries. Become fluent with them by studying the basic layouts, positions, and meanings. Then practice the spreads on your own questions in a reading for yourself before interpreting the layout for others. Your subconscious is accustomed to communicating with you in a certain pattern—i.e., a certain style of card spread. When you change or add a new layout, it needs time to acclimate.

Here are three various reading styles. These readings are also featured in detail in Part II.

- **The Whole Self** layout answers special questions highlighting the idea of personal responsibility and self-awareness.

- **The Zodiac** layout is useful when Seekers require information on a variety of topics; usually involves a six-month to one-year time period and blends predictions with self-awareness.

- **The Four Seasons** layout is a short-term, predictive layout performed on the yearly quadrants of spring, summer, autumn, and winter; also includes a spiritual dimension.

FUN WAYS TO UNDERSTAND THE TAROT

Why should learning the Tarot be all memorization, interpretation, and study? Most people learn by doing and creative play, so I have developed some unconventional fun-filled ways to increase your Tarot knowledge. This section also includes classical Tarot events and projects you can enjoy that are guaranteed to increase your understanding of the cards.

The Tarot Scavenger Hunt

For this activity, you need digital cameras or other instant-photo devices, a deck of Tarot cards, and a location like a mall, a home, a village neighborhood, or an outdoor area. Place the Tarot deck inside a box or bag. Ask each person to choose five cards and give them one hour to photograph their interpretation of the cards chosen. The person who photographs all their cards in the shortest time wins.

Variations: Give each person the same cards. The person who photographs the best representation of them as voted by the group is the winner. Or the person who comes up with a photographic representation the fastest is the winner. Another option is to divide the group into two teams and choose cards in increased levels of difficulty. Each team gives the other the chosen cards after each round at prearranged time intervals. The team that produces the best image for each card wins.

For example, if you decide to have your scavenger hunt in a mall, the people and store mannequins can represent the Court cards; various situations or stores may portray the Minor Arcana; offices, service or other facilities may represent the Major Arcana. A maternity clothing store may represent The Empress, while an attorney's office may represent the Justice Arcanum. You may find suitable images for the Ace of Swords in the knife department; the Seven of Cups may be seven stacked drinking glasses; a woman reading a book may be the Queen of Swords; a child pitching coins or asking for a donation to charity may be the Page of Pentacles; a young man in the athletics department choosing a baseball bat may be the Knight of Wands. The possibilities are endless!

Giving yourself the opportunity to think in this creative way will enhance your Tarot repertoire, whether you play the scavenger hunt game or simply use this mode of observation when traveling, socializing, or engaging with your everyday world in an imaginative way.

The Mystery Message Puzzle

For this activity, you will need small, blank jigsaw puzzles available in most arts-and-craft stores, water-based paints, and brushes. Have each individual in the Tarot group draw the name of another person in the group; keep the names secret. Then have everyone choose a favorable Tarot card for their secret person. The card selected should be a representation of their current circumstances, or that which is coming into prominence in their life. For example, if a person is about to take on more power in his or her job, choose The Emperor; if someone is receiving a spiritual initiation, the Temperance card is appropriate; if new money, a new business, or a new home is on the horizon, choose the Ace of Pentacles. Each selection requires that the participants know the cards and can translate their fellow participants' current life into an appropriate Tarot representation.

Then have each person paint a version of the card on the jigsaw puzzle; make sure they each leave room around the periphery for a special message based on the card that they will compose for their secret partners. For example, for The Emperor, paint his staff or another symbol of the card and design a message like: "You will have well-deserved empowerment," or "Power and mastery are yours."

Allow time for each puzzle to dry, then break it up, place the pieces in an envelope, and mail it to or exchange it with your secret partner. In this way, each participant gives and receives a message and has fun designing and putting one together. This enhances their Tarot knowledge by making them explain their choice and their interpretation to their secret person. The Mystery Puzzle works something like the fortune-cookie messages we tend to cherish. It provides encouragement and hope, which is always worthwhile in Tarot work.

The Gourmet Tarot House-hopping Party

Your Tarot group will have great fun incorporating food and drink with the cards. You can have a house gathering to which each person brings a dish to share, or you can "house-hop" for each course of the Tarot meal.

Place the Temperance card and the four Aces from your deck in an envelope. Have each person choose a card. This represents the kind of food and dining implements they will contribute, based on the card's elemental attribution (Wands for fire; Cups for water; Swords for air; Pentacles for earth). If there are more than five people, you can create teams; if there are fewer than five, you'll have to double up or eliminate food categories.

The person who picks the Temperance card will be the baker. An alternate title for Temperance is The Alchemist, and baking is true alchemy that requires precision, mixing, and timing. Pentacles represent the platter in medieval legends, therefore the plates and platters will be supplied by the person who draws the Ace of Pentacles. Cups are obvious—but don't forget the bowls. Swords represent cutlery, especially knives, skewers, and fondue forks. Wands, which are associated with heat, correlate to the actual stove, oven, barbecue, or other cooking method.

The person who draws the Ace of Wands supplies hot, spicy foods, as well as those cooked over an open flame. So the person who draws the Ace of Cups will supply all beverages and foods from the sea—anything from seaweed sushi to seafood—as well as liquids like soups, sauces, and gravies. The person who draws the Ace of Swords may supply a roasted bird beautifully and skillfully carved (Swords relate to knives and skill), skewered vegetables or fruits, or a fondue. The person who draws the Ace of Pentacles may bring beautiful platters filled with fruits and vegetables—especially grapes, as they appear numerous times in the Pentacles illustrations.

You can extend the Tarot theme of your dinner party through colors, flowers, candles, and music. Dress according to the suit you've chosen in color and style, and consider music that reflects the mood of the suits to accompany each course! Tarot charades is a good way to end your dinner party, with individuals acting out different Tarot cards and participants guessing which card is being portrayed.

Another classic Tarot event is the costume party. Ask each person to dress as a favored card character and take on the character qualities portrayed in the image. This practice has a strong basis in magical and ritual practices, where the special colors, styles, symbols, and regalia are worn to invoke and evoke desired qualities.

You may want to experiment with this practice outside a party atmosphere using the card's colors. For example, if you want to create an atmosphere of purity and integrity, wear the High Priestess's colors. The colors of the Cups cards will bring love, tranquility, and trust; Swords associate with intelligence, decisiveness, and clarity;

Wands represent courage, desire, and will; Pentacles speak to prosperity and rich resources. It helps to experiment with this practice, because it yields the best results when you feel comfortable with it, encouraging other people to respond positively to you.

Another classic Tarot project is scrapbooking. With the wide array of scrapbook resources available, you can create a Tarot version using colors, images that represent the deck, actual favorite Tarot cards, and text, poetry, and lyrics. This is a way to share, collect, and archive all your favorite Tarot material from your readings and personal journaling.

Enhancing a Party with the Tarot Cards

Here are some unique suggestions for using the Tarot cards to enhance your parties.

The Birthday Wish: Place ten candles in firm holders on a table. Under each, place a favorable Tarot card facedown. Light the candles and have one person close his or her eyes and blow out some of the candles. Read the cards under the candles that have been blown out. Replace the cards, relight the candles, and repeat for each individual. Consider a Tarot-card birthday cake. You can have a photo of a card placed on the top or make your own version of a card.

The Valentine Party: This works best for a sit-down dinner, lunch, or breakfast. Decorate a shoe box with Valentine themes; make a slit in the top of the box. Place romantic Tarot cards inside the box and use it as a centerpiece. Before your guests arrive, set the table, placing more romantic cards under each place setting. Use The Lovers, The Empress, The Magician, The Emperor, The Star, The Sun, and The World, as well as the Cups Court cards and the Ace, Two, Three, Six, Nine, and Ten of Cups.

The key is that you do not know who will sit where. Just tell everyone to sit wherever they wish for the meal. After everyone is settled, announce that a special message awaits each person under his or her plate. The interpretation and subsequent sharing of life stories prompted by the cards will give everyone a great source of conversation for the meal. You can ask each diner to share his or her card and invite comments from the others. Afterward, invite each guest to reach inside the Valentine box for an additional Tarot-card message of love.

When you enjoy your interaction with the cards from a pleasurable event, it serves to balance the usual emphasis on the intellectual and intuitive approach. The earthly and sensate side of the cards and their message can be emphasized by the creation of a room, altar, art, fashion, or garden based on the cards' designs. The more ways you incorporate the cards into your life, the deeper an understanding you'll have of the Tarot.

READING FOR OTHERS

When you perform readings for other people, you sharpen your interpretive skills. You attain a deepened understanding of the inner workings of the Tarot through sharing the cards' messages. As you communicate with the deck for others, you also open and maintain a line of contact with your Higher Self.

The best practice for witnessing how the cards function on a predictive level is to form a Tarot group. Each member can bring to the group a willing participant—someone known only to them. The other members can read for the volunteers and receive feedback. Reading for each other—studying, recording, and assessing your predictions over a period of time—will accelerate your confidence in your own delineation skills.

Try volunteering to read for a fund-raising event. You'll encounter a variety of situations that will test your skills for rapid interpretations. Or have a gathering or home party at which you perform mini-Tarot readings for practice with people that you do not know well. I recommend starting with small gatherings of two to four people and reading for fifteen to twenty minutes. Make sure the consultations are private.

Some restaurants invite readers to work on off-nights, and New Age or occult bookstores also welcome readers. Psychic fairs and expos also offer quick, intense reading opportunities. In these scenarios, you have to be fast, accurate, articulate, confident, and kind.

Recently, I began to read for a psychic reading phone line service. Time is money in that venue. Connecting with the client, asking a question, then shuffling and laying out the cards is far too time consuming and tends to discourage business. Instead, I simply shuffled the cards and lay them out prior to the client's phone call. I ask my spiritual teachers to guide the person who belongs to the reading to call me. The method works beautifully.

Phone readings accelerate your analytical skills. Simply lay out the cards in your favorite spread. You and your fellow students can assess what the caller is asking about, and then look at the future cards for predictions.

When the caller telephones and asks you his or her question, you immediately see how the reading already in front of you describes the situation. This procedure is a great learning tool, teaching how the cards actually reveal their messages. You can quickly build confidence as you instantly hear whether your assessment is correct, incorrect, or needs modification or explanation.

Another fascinating way to develop your interpretive skill is through current events. Choose a political, entertainment, or sports topic, and perform readings about the progression of events. Try inquiring about a celebrity's situation, or even ask about the unfolding drama in one of your favorite television programs. This practice provides the opportunity to read characters' personalities and predict events.

For current-events readings, simply shuffle the cards and focus on a question like, "What does the President's future look like in the election campaign?" or "Show me the outcome of the tennis match this week." Record the cards and your predictions. Think about how you would explain the reading to the subject. This practice is guaranteed to boost your confidence level.

All these practices and circumstances will reveal how you feel when reading for a wide variety of people—strangers, friends, or coworkers. Take note of your feelings. Do you feel drained? Impatient? Positive? Negative? These reactions will reflect your strengths and those areas where you need to develop coping strategies that can be discussed in a group.

After each reading, review. Ask yourself when you received most of the information. Was it in the beginning of the session? After the cards were laid out? In conversation with the person? During the actual interpretation? Or even before the session began?

Analyze when your reader's intuition is strongest, then watch for the timing in subsequent sessions. By knowing your strongest psychic timing, you'll learn to trust the flow and expand your focus, allowing more promptings to be revealed. The best practice is to develop your own rhythm and style; do not try to imitate other readers.

PSYCHIC INTRUSION

The ability to connect with another person's energy field and retrieve relevant information is part of the energy dynamic of a reading. While this practice helps you gather psychic information, it can produce a draining effect known as psychic intrusion. The hallmark of this unfortunate side effect is a feeling that other people are draining your energy.

It can also sometimes result from an individual attaching themselves to you psychically through his or her unresolved unconscious emotions. If you find yourself feeling burned out, preoccupied with an individual's problem you discussed during a reading, and/or unable to focus on and direct your will toward your own well-being, you may be experiencing psychic intrusion.

If you have an empathetic or sympathetic disposition, this may make you prone to psychic intrusion, whether consciously through your intuition or simply by being in an environment of emotional conflict. I refer to this as becoming a psychic sponge. This state of imbalance doesn't help you or the other person. It leaves you sapped of energy and uninterested in your own spiritual progression.

I have experienced psychic intrusion in a variety of ways. The worst examples occurred when I actually awakened from a dream about reading for strangers throughout the night. This wasn't just my mind processing readings I had already performed for other people. The dream featured strangers; their souls were actually receiving readings from me during sleep. My psychic energy was available because I had neglected to protect and purify it, and the souls of the other people recognized that and gravitated to me without my conscious consent.

The example that stands out the most for me occurred when I dreamed about giving a reading for a new client and then had the actual person appear for a session the following day. The dream was obviously precognitive, yet I felt violated when I considered it in the context of the many other dreams of strangers I was experiencing. All the evidence pointed to me being an open channel. Clearly I needed to purify and protect my energy field more effectively.

Here is an effective technique I use for all intrusion situations. This practice will remove unwanted energies, protect you, and restore your balance.

The Ace of Cups Astral Scan

When you start this meditation practice, you may become aware of memories, surprising energy attached to you from other people, and even past-life information. You'll also recognize where you are vulnerable in your energy body and learn ways to increase protection for the area. As you integrate the Astral Scan into your regular routine, less material will surface that needs to be purified.

Prepare your meditation environment in a style that is comfortable for you. This may include candles, incense, flowers, spiritual/religious icons, a special chalice with pure water, a crystal, a wand, and your Tarot deck. You may want to play special music.

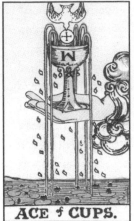

ACE ⚡ CUPS.

Make sure that you will be undisturbed for at least twenty to thirty minutes. You may also want to have a journal and pen readily available.

Begin by placing the Ace of Cups from your favorite deck in front of you at eye level. The focus for this meditation is the portion of the card illustration that depicts the water or waves emitting from the top of the chalice in the illustration. Take a minute to center your mind on that area.

Take a few deep breaths and look at the water spouting like a fountain and flowing downward. This depicts the actual procedure of our practice. Now focus on the top of your head. Feel it become soft. Gently open, then sense, imagine, or hear the water flowing out of the opening.

Imagine a stream of clear light-filled water flowing from your head in rivulets, from top to bottom. Repeat this process, moving around your body until you reach the starting point. Another way to focus on the practice is to use your hand to simulate the sweeping of your energy field from head to toe. This will clean your aura of unwanted psychic intrusions, and of attachments from others and the past.

During the process, you may sense an area that feels clogged, cold, stagnant, or otherwise out of balance. Stop at that area and ask to be shown what you need to know about the energy shift. A past or present person, prior experience, or even a past-life memory that is clinging to you may spring to mind.

You may be prompted to place your hands at that area and move them in a certain way, in a brushing or a pulling motion. Let your intuition be your guide with these movements. Release the person, memory, or past life by seeing the discharged energy encapsulated in a ball of light that you toss into the Great Sea of Understanding (a place of dissolution and no return). The sea is also pictured in the Ace of Cups.

Finally, purify your energy. Let it radiate, wash, or beam across the location where you stopped with white light. Picture it sealing the area of vulnerability.

Continue with the practice until you reach the starting point. Allow a few minutes to sit in the new cleansed, restored energy field. Ask that this state of balance remain with you. Additional information may then be revealed about the meditation. You may make requests or suggestions at this juncture. Review the experience while still in this altered, expanded state of mind before you return to your daily activities.

End the meditation by imagining your entire body encapsulated in pure gold, white, or crystal light that is clear, impenetrable, and pure. This puts you in contact with the best spiritual and intuitive energies and leaves you protected from vibrations that do not serve the best and highest good. Focus once more at the top of your head and see the streams of water revert back inside you, as if the fountain were turned off. Now close the top, sealing it with extra white light. Return to normal consciousness by breathing in your usual rhythm.

After the meditation, consider topics for discussion or journaling, including a new awareness of where you may have an energy leak or are vulnerable. This may be in the front or back of your body, or in your chakra centers. Some individuals discover that their most precious psychic instrument, their third eye, is clogged with intrusive debris. Others find their solar plexus, throat, or other areas are in need of purification, protection, and closing. I have found that past-life and unconscious material of all kinds can be attached to the back.

Spend a few minutes radiating intense white light to the area and see it sealed and purified. This is the best way to ensure that the intrusion is a thing of the past. The best practice is to clean your energy field routinely after intense reading experiences, before advising for others, and when performing spiritual practices. This is a dandy method for ridding yourself of unwanted attachments from people or your past, and traumatic experiences that need releasing.

At times during a session, you may feel that the person you are advising needs to understand this special practice. The cards that may signal this to you are the reversed Ace, Page, Queen, Knight, and King of Cups; the Seven of Cups; and reversed Two, Three, and Six of Cups. Negative Sword cards; The Magician, High Priestess, Empress, or Hanged Man reversed; and the upright Moon may also be significant.

Offer to explain the conundrum of psychic intrusion to your clients. If they are ready to be proactive, they will ask what can be done to correct the situation. Explain the Ace of Cups Astral Scan practice and offer to share the technique with them. One of the most wonderful aspects of this practice is the shift in awareness you can give to Seekers, guiding them to realize they have a choice and a remedy for unwanted intrusion by others.

More practices for aligning with sacred energies, releasing the past, and creating protection are given in Part III of this book. You'll find ways to connect with your spiritual helpers, sever karmic patterns, and much more. The questions, affirmations, and meditations for each Major Arcanum will help you foster your soul growth and guide others.

The best Tarot interpreters are centered in their souls, receiving information to share in readings for themselves and others from the Higher Self. They practice meditation, journal, and use affirmations to foster a relationship with their spiritual source. The practices in Part III will develop your spiritual nature. This is the greatest way for the power of the Tarot to work through you for the benefit of yourself and other people.

PART TWO

THREE NEW TAROT SPREADS

One of the most effective ways to enhance your interpretive skill is to study how a professional reader creates a succinct interpretation of the Tarot's messages for a Seeker. The ongoing challenge of incorporating a card's meaning with its placement in a layout is explained in this section. Here, we'll explore methods for card interpretation step-by-step. I have chosen three Tarot spreads in this section, and I include information about each card's explanation. We'll also use the Daath cards, another important aspect of card divination, to find additional information.

·4·

THE ZODIAC SPREAD

The Zodiac Spread features the classic map of life, pictured as a diagram of twelve sections within a wheel representing spiritual wholeness and cycles of time. You should blend the meanings of your cards with the corresponding life sector meaning for predictions and insights for twelve life topics. Because the astrology chart design is an ancient pattern imprinted on humanity's psyche, the Higher Self will easily communicate its guidance to you using the recognizable archetypal wheel format.

THE LAYOUT

The Zodiac Tarot spread is a wonderful classical layout that provides answers to a wide variety of life questions. It examines the twelve departments of life as defined by the Zodiac wheel and the meaning of the twelve houses of astrology. Begin by placing the following cards in the Zodiac layout, as illustrated in the diagram on page 74.

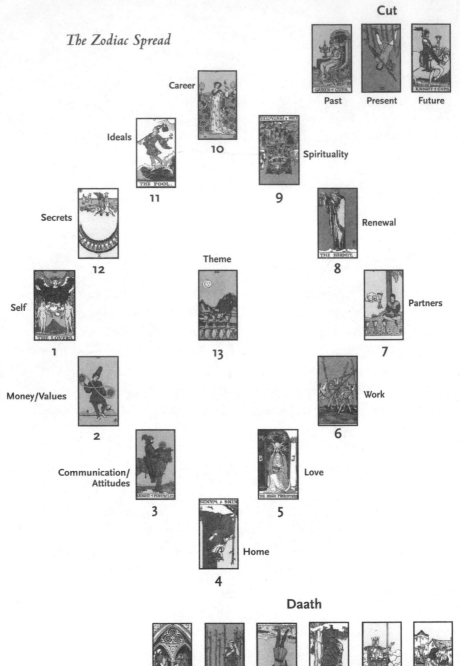

The Zodiac Spread

Cut

Past   Present   Future

Career

10

Ideals

11

Spirituality

9

Secrets

12

Renewal

8

Self

1

Theme

13

Partners

7

Money/Values

2

Work

6

Communication/
Attitudes

3

Love

5

Home

4

Daath

Cut:

Past	Queen of Cups
Present	Seven of Wands reversed
Future	Knight of Cups

Layout:

House 1	The Lovers—self
House 2	Two of Pentacles—values, money
House 3	Knight of Pentacles—mind & communication
House 4	King of Wands Reversed—home
House 5	The High Priestess—love
House 6	Five of Wands—work
House 7	Four of Cups—partners
House 8	The Hermit—renewal
House 9	King of Pentacles reversed—spirituality
House 10	Nine of Pentacles—career
House 11	The Fool—ideals
House 12	Ten of Cups reversed—secrets
Position 13	Eight of Cups—theme & summary

Daath:

The Daath cards are the seven cards that follow any style of layout. They are placed in sequence, one through seven, after the primary layout has been dealt. For this reading, the Daath cards are as follows:

D1	Three of Pentacles
D2	Nine of Wands
D3	Page of Pentacles reversed
D4	Three of Cups reversed
D5	Queen of Swords
D6	Six of Cups
D7	Knight of Cups
+	The Moon reversed

Since the final card (number 7) is a Court card, another card is drawn and laid out to reveal further information about the character. The Daath, (translated as "hidden" or "occult information") is read in conjunction with the main spread. The seven cards provide details, confirmation, and additional insights regarding the main focus of the reading.

If you judge the Daath to have a theme dissimilar to the content of the main reading, you can safely assume that the cards are commenting on a second important question for the Seeker to consider. Interpret the first cards in the sequence as past, middle cards as present, and last cards as future. The Daath's message may be given during the main reading or after. In this example, we see a happy, secure future for her love life (Six of Cups, Knight of Cups, and a reversed Moon). This supports and confirms the main Zodiac Spread message.

THE CUT

The Queen of Cups appears in the past placement, the Seven of Wands reversed appears in the present placement, and the Knight of Cups appears in the future placement.

The Queen of Cups in the past describes the Seeker's nature. She has an emotional nature and is sensitive, intuitive, and nurturing. Her strength is faith in love. Currently, she is feeling nonconfrontational, after having courageously confronted difficult circumstances; this interpretation is denoted by the reversed Seven of Wands.

The Knight of Cups in the future suggests a male influence of a trustworthy nature. He will open his heart to her, and her faith will be restored. A positive turning point for the affairs of the heart is predicted.

SAMPLE READING

In this reading, the client is a woman who has inquired about the next six months—we'll call her Hannah. Note the five Major Arcana in the layout—The Lovers in the first house, The High Priestess in the fifth house, The Hermit in the eighth house, and The Fool in the eleventh house. The Moon reversed is the final card of the Daath.

The Major Arcana represent Hannah's significant life lessons and the spiritual energies available to her. The Zodiac houses, or divisions in which they appear, denote which life aspects are experiencing these influences—in our example, self in the first house, love in the fifth, renewal in the eighth, and ideals in the eleventh. The Knight of Pentacles appears in the third house, suggesting a turning point (Knights denote turning points) regarding manifestation (the Pentacles realm) and third-house subjects of communication, consciousness, and learning.

The Daath also concludes with another Knight, coupled with a Major Arcana. A turning point regarding an emotional matter (Knight of Cups) is therefore forecast (the final cards in the Daath represent the future) with a significant outcome (The Moon reversed) indicating a positive change and honest love.

Analysis of the distribution of suits (including the Daath) reveals eight Cups, six Pentacles, four Wands, and one Sword. This suggests that Cup and Pentacle matters (i.e., love, faith, and emotional, practical, and real-life situations) will figure most prominently in Hannah's life.

The theme of the reading, The Eight of Cups in position Thirteen reveals an emotional disappointment leading to soul searching and the tending to the quest and journey to align with the true self. This unhappiness is confirmed in the twelfth house of secrets, the Ten of Cups reversed.

Her home life, read from the fourth house, shows a man who's selfish behavior is making her miserable, the reversed King of Wands. Even her spiritual life is hampered by the dull, possessive nature of this man; his presence reappears as the reversed King of Pentacles in the ninth house of Spirituality.

The Lovers card appears in the first house—the house of the self. The first house reveals that which is coming into consciousness, the life experience and realization that are currently being initiated.

Hannah is beginning to experience (first house) personal healing, integration, and balance between mind and emotions, spirit and matter (The Lovers). Correct discrimination and choice-making based on this new balance (The Lovers) will also be initiated (first house). She may also experience (first house) a love relationship of a true, healing, and meaningful nature (The Lovers). The Archangel Raphael confers healing and a blessed union upon her.

Hannah may be on the cusp of a soul-centered life with a spiritual renewal. The Archangel Raphael, depicted in The Lovers, represents initiation into a balanced, whole relationship, both within her nature and in the external world.

The Two of Pentacles turned up in the house of values, money, possessions, earning ability, and talents. Successful, well-balanced organization of Hannah's finances (second house) is indicated. Monies will fluctuate within the expected normal bounds. She will be able to handle the changing circumstances due to her confident, adept management skills (Two of Pentacles).

Hannah has more than one talent or skill (second house) for income generation. This is indicated by the two pentacles, or economic sources, pictured in the card. Earning ability will be derived from two sources or may be cyclical. The ships in the illustration's background indicate Hannah's material treasures. Her possessions will be tended to conscientiously and with care (Two of Pentacles). Any purchases will be well-thought-out and budgeted in keeping with her values of spending within reason. She values and possesses the capacity to anticipate her economic situation, and there will be monies to work with.

The Knight of Pentacles appears in the house of communication, consciousness, siblings, and learning experiences. If Hannah had a brother, the interpretation would be that the sibling's future forecast around finances, work security, and health is stable. An important matter regarding communication (i.e., written or spoken word) will yield tangible results through hard work (Knight of Pentacles). A positive financial turning point may occur through her well-organized communication ability (third house). Hannah is a writer (communication) who may experience the successful manifestation of a project. A short journey (third house) of a practical, work, health, or real-estate nature may also be indicated. A reliable man (Knight of Pentacles) connected with the communications industry may be part of Hannah's life for the upcoming time period.

Her work life is stressed as indicated by the Five of Wands in the sixth house of work. However, she is clear about her sincere intentions and willingness to bravely assert herself.

Her career house, the tenth house, has the Nine of Pentacles, the guidance is to heed her own intuition and develop long term security through cultivating her talents and strengths during turbulent times (Five of Wands, Two of Pentacles)

Her soul self, the High Priestess, Queen of Cups, Eight of Cups and reversed Moon, takes precedence in the reading. The newfound balance and choice of freedom (The Fool and Lovers) liberates her from an oppressive man, the reversed Kings of Wands and Pentacles.

Hannah will thrive during the next six months through choosing to take a correct leap of faith (The Fool, The Lovers) toward true love, the Knight of Cups and The Lovers.

I couldn't help but feel that the Hermit's lantern was lighting her path toward fulfillment and that the High Priestess, knowing Hannah's soul purpose was approving and blessing her choices.

·5·

THE WHOLE SELF
SPREAD

The design of a Whole Self reading is based on the ancient symbol of the circle with a dot in the center. The circle represents wholeness, cycles, completeness, and time enclosing space, as well as timelessness. The dot in the center represents the quintessence of the authentic Self.

Use this layout for self-understanding, decision-making, and consciousness-raising when seeking guidance about a significant aspect of life. The reading will describe the personality qualities used in tending to the subject. More important, it will reveal the whole self—in other words, hidden resources, the purpose for the challenge, meaningful lessons, and what to do to achieve your aims. Once delineated, these qualities will guide you toward empowerment regarding the topic of your inquiry.

Since real change begins from within, it is important that you fully understand the various aspects of your being available for your empowerment. The Whole Self reading provides self-awareness on all five levels of the psyche: the ego, subconscious, body (doing), soul, and quintessence. The quintessence is the link with spirit and is represented by the Aces. With these aptitudes defined by the cards, you can bring new power to the inquiry and truly make progress. You may want to explore a "stuck" or difficult-to-understand, challenging life area for this spread.

The cards used for the reading are the four Aces and the sixteen Court cards. The Court represents character traits and identity. All their meanings are provided in this chapter. The King, Queen, Knight, and Page are regarded as distinct aspects of your complete or whole self. The Whole Self reading focuses on the "who" of the Tarot cards, providing an extra way to increase your Tarot vocabulary for the Court cards. It also suggests that the Court cards represent various functions in your being. The Ace reveals the soul, heart, and essence of the matter, and appears in Position 1. The King reveals the way you think of yourself and your personality expression and appears in Position 2. The Queen reveals your unconscious beliefs and powers you can utilize and appears in Position 3. The Knight represents the initiation, lesson, challenge, or triumph you face and appears in Position 4. The Page denotes action to take to create empowerment and appears in Position 5.

THE LAYOUT

Decide on the subject for the reading. Choose one with a challenging quality, or a theme of change and personal empowerment. Separate the Pages, Knights, Queens, Kings, and Aces from the deck. You will use only these cards. Place them in five piles of four cards each. The cards should be both upright and reversed because you have thoroughly mixed and shuffled them.

Shuffle the Aces and fan them facedown. Then pass your left hand over the pile, pick one, and place it in the Ace position, facedown. Repeat the procedure with Kings in Position 2, the Queens in Position 3, the Knights in Position 4, and the Pages in Position 5 (see diagram). You will have a total of five cards to interpret in this reading.

Turn over all five cards and determine if a dominant suit has appeared, or if there is one suit that is entirely missing, or if two suits are almost perfectly balanced. Note: If a suit is not present, pay special attention, since it is the messages contained in that suit and its corresponding element that need most to be integrated

The Whole Self Spread

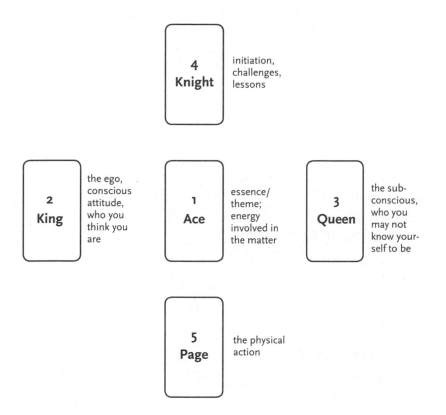

Ace: Divine forces, spiritual essence, spiritual solution, healing agent, energy, virtue

King: The ego, conscious attitude, who you think you are

Queen: The subconscious, who you may not know yourself to be, and powers to utilize

Knight: Initiation, lesson, challenge, triumph

Page: Action to undertake to create empowerment

concerning the matter at hand. For example, if no Swords appear, study and apply the meanings of the suit and the Ace, King, Queen, Knight, and Page for guidance and recommended actions. In this example, an absence of Swords indicates a need to be just, true, have integrity, be analytical, and clearheaded.

Sometimes, a layout may be filled entirely or almost entirely with one suit. This also points directly to the message contained in the meaning of the suit. Read the meanings of each suit below and review the information presented in the reading interpretation section for ways to address the question and take action.

Wands: Courageous, empowering, creating, leading, aspiring, ambitious, true nature, real-feeling self. Energy and will.

Cups: Nurturing, imagining, caring, loving, intuition, soul messages. Openheartedness. Faithful.

Swords: Integrity, learning, intellect, communication, mental fortitude, constructive attitude, discipline, analysis, and observation. Open-mindedness.

Pentacles: Labors of love. Gathering, cultivating, grounding, making, manifesting, and establishing. Practicality. Charitable. Gifts and talents utilized.

If the card is reversed, the qualities described are in need of integration.

POSITION INTERPRETATION

The positions of the cards in the layout influence the meaning of the card in the reading.

Position 1. The Ace

Read the Ace as the type of energy involved, the theme of the matter, and also as divine forces at work. The Ace, or quintessence, is the spiritual essence. The card represents a specific virtue and how the Infinite Intelligence is working through the question you've asked. It is also the solution, the origin of the lesson, and the healing agent.

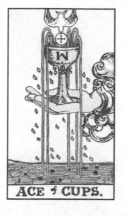

Ace of Wands: Courageous, empowering, creating, leading, aspiring, ambitious, true nature, real-feeling self. Energy and will.

Ace of Cups: Nurturing, imagining, caring, loving, intuition, soul messages. Openheartedness. Faithful.

Ace of Swords: Integrity, learning, intellect, communication, mental fortitude, constructive attitude, discipline, analysis, and observation. Open-mindedness.

Ace of Pentacles: Labors of love. Gathering, cultivating, grounding, making, manifesting, and establishing. Practicality. Charitable. Gifts and talents utilized.

Position 2. The King

The King reveals attitude and identity—how you see or approach the matter. The King shows how the situation is currently viewed and judged. He represents the personal conscious awareness and values regarding the question. The King is the aspect of yourself that represents your established ego structure; he is how you present yourself to the world. This placement denotes the cultivated, developed part of the self and who you consciously know yourself to be, whether male or female.

King of Wands: Feels what is right, handles his feelings with appropriate and natural order in life; interested in relationships; extroverted; strong sense of life purpose, of truth based on values; has style; loves beauty, can distinguish what is important and act courageously. Trusts spontaneous feelings without losing sight of values, of friendship, family, or love. Standards of judgment based on cooperation, win-win situation; enthusiasm, honesty, achievement. Focuses upon what constitutes success for him and others, i.e., what can be achieved.

Reversed: Intolerant, egomaniacal; bully, bossy, judgmental, angry; antics that are theatrical and attention-seeking. Needs to be loved and supported by others, however is unclear about ambitions and what matters to him.

King of Cups: Receives hunches; thinks about the future and sees the meaning behind and within a situation. Imaginative, has faith in the unseen realms. Creative, can envision and create but doesn't necessarily stay to reap. Perceives the whole picture; asks why, seeks meaning, cherishes wisdom, and is insightful. Sensitive, looks at all the creative possibilities, intuits situation with a visionary style that begets a metaphor capturing its essence. Offers astute observations and advice. Asks, "Why is this happening?" Wants to understand, seeks wisdom and insights. Gentle, loving, nurturing, compassionate.

Reversed: Viewpoint that is too emotional, armored, defensive, or in denial; filled with addictions and indulgences. Self-deceptive, delusional; emotionality clouds judgment, unable to be loving toward others or himself. Cannot listen to feelings and nurture through gentle, compassionate means. Undisciplined, emotionally troubled behavior.

King of Swords: Explains things with ease, asks "how does it function?" Loves theory, facts of the matter. Fairness and action with integrity. Instinctive and direct viewpoint, says what he means, clear analysis; gets to the point, has the stance of perfection because he has situation completely assessed in realistic terms; good objective judgment. Cool, authoritative; opinions based on theory and "how" something functions; truth, classifies information.

Reversed: Cold, judgmental, superior, and moralizing; inhuman, prejudiced; inaccurate assessment.

King of Pentacles: Asks, "What is it?" Image is important, sensation, observes detail, awareness of here and now, taste, touch, etc. Manual work and physical experience are soul-making. Aware of what is occurring inside himself, bodily sensations. Able to give to others. Labors of love are of value. Talented, gifted; well-expressed aptitudes have brought him substance and wealth.

Reasonable, realistic, detailed assessment regarding facts of what is occurring; values, security, continuity; organized, goal-oriented; applies himself, gets to work; "working on it" approach, industriousness. He senses information, receives gut feelings and hunches, but needs to value asking their meaning.

Reversed: Unreasonable, controlling, unimaginative; fearful of losing; in denial, unwilling to take control.

Position 3. The Queen

The Queen reveals the subconscious self and powers. Messages from the soul, information of which the Seeker may be unaware about his or her potential self, past, or future, secretly held beliefs for good or ill, and subconscious feelings about the matter.

When she appears reversed, this indicates an imbalance. The Queen of Cups or Pentacles reversed can be too passive, unable to focus and know and act on desires. The Queen of Wands or Swords reversed appears when there is too much action, forcing, and not enough reflection.

Queen of Wands: Radiance. Strength of character, fusion of feminine and masculine qualities, relationship, either internal (i.e., with spiritual unfoldment, ambition, etc.) or external, producing power, creativity, love, attraction, and individuality. Solar soul capacity to radiate or emanate. Energy worker can transmit and receive messages through energy "fields." Soul self, intention, will; courage and passion toward spiritual knowing; desires the spirit of love to enflame her. Empowered through becoming her true nature and developing her potentials, letting love lead the way. She possesses the magical soul and charismatic power of radiance due to her capacity to feel and emanate. Has a power similar to The Empress.

QUEEN ♂ WANDS.

Reversed: Unable to direct her will successfully, she becomes frustrated and angry.

Queen of Cups: Joy. Must have faith and healthy emotional life; a deep capacity to imagine, create, intuit, and delve into the subconscious waters. Heart ideally open and released from negative past. Higher Self, imagination, and intuition create a channel for soul information where her being becomes a vessel for the divine. State of opening to receive through creation of tranquility. Desires to become a channel for the gift of the spirit. Empowered through purifying her emotional energy and practicing deep trance, contemplation, and meditative states. Has a sim-  ilar power to The High Priestess. Lunar soul worker. Is connected to the great universal sea of the collective unconscious. May be highly involved with soul level and only be partially aware of its magnitude. At her finest when interacting with information from dreams or meditation, or in response to nurturing a creative project inspired by family, relationship, or personal expression of meaningful contribution.

Reversed: Energy field clogged with toxic emotional debris, she has no way to open her heart and receive her soul.

Queen of Swords: Dissolution and closure, a capacity to grow with and through adversity and change. Knows how to "get over it and get on with it." Deep awareness of her strong intellect, positive attitude; philosophical way of perceiving the meaning of a situation. Astute psychologist, perceives the thoughts behind events, especially unproductive ones. Soul and psyche are represented by her butterfly crown;

she understands the precept "change your mind and you will change your life." Her mental discipline attains clarity of mind and movement into heightened states of awareness, such as planes of genius, information, wisdom, and invention. Seeks to share the knowledge with others. Values personal integrity and communication with others to inform, enlighten, and inspire.

Reversed: Bitterness and dwelling on details of disappointment, an unproductive judgmental attitude. The mind becomes an agent for destruction; actions are fraught with combat and self-betrayal.

QUEEN of PENTACLES

Queen of Pentacles: Concretization. Established in strength, her soul is expressed through caring and tending to the home, career, family, garden, body, and health. Labors of love are of value, as are charitable involvements. Her rich talents yield ample abundance. Practices ceremony and rituals; gives of herself and her bounty to others, lends a helping hand with her resources, which may be derived from her position, prosperity, or influential connections. On the soul level, a sensual woman involved with nature and its spiritual essence of healing, harmony, and teaching. She is in "sync" with the energy of the seasons and weather. Has strong affinity to sacred places and structures, receiving subtle messages through them. Spirituality found in nature, earthy types of worship; native, pagan, Celtic, aboriginal cultures connected to the environment and land. Blends spirit and matter by utilizing yoga, Tai Chi, healing body therapies, sacred dance, and movement. Expresses soul through cultivation of talents, helping others access their resources; protects and preserves that which is of value.

Reversed: Ungrounded, out of touch with sense and body, needs to come down to earth or may be overly involved with exterior self and materialism. Vanity, body worship, or feeding self-esteem through image, power, and possessions. Excesses in the monetary realm with loss of inner content and soul. Impractical, unrealistic, and irresponsible.

Position 4. The Knight

This is a position of initiation, challenge, triumphs, and lessons involved with the inquiry. Ideas associated with the Knight include the quest, the hero, honor, and battle. When you don the knightly armor, you do battle with your lower self—for example, your fears. You overcome them, not through ignoring them, but by facing the adversary within and outside you and conquering through faith in yourself and your connection with your Higher Self's teachings and powers. Knights are triumphant at handling a test, a challenge, lessons, and initiations involving the appropriate handling of will (Wands), love (Cups), force (Swords), and tangible possessions (Pentacles).

Reversed: All the Knights reversed indicates a misuse or misdirection of the corresponding elemental challenge. The Knight of Wands reversed is a misuse of ambition. The Knight of Cups reversed is a misuse of faith to deceive. The Knight of Swords reversed is a misuse of mental acumen closed-mindedness. The Knight of Pentacles reversed is a misuse of talent and resources, money, and possessions.

Knight of Wands: Element of fire; spirit and its personality vehicle are triumphantly dedicated to its true will and growing the authentic self. Courage and fortitude in direction of genuine aspiration.

KNIGHT of WANDS

Knight of Cups: Element of water; challenge to have and sustain a relationship with faith in the power of love, creativity, imagination, and the soulful life. Challenge to remain dedicated to impressions and intuitive knowing from the inner self; flows with sensitive response to the external world, then creates a heartfelt response. Triumphant engagement of romantic, soulful essence, honoring it and expressing it in a meaningful form; loving or creating.

KNIGHT of CUPS.

Knight of Swords: Element of air; intellect over passion; triumphant forging of own values and attitudes resulting in action and decision-making. Channeling of higher intelligence and spiritual heart forged into productive purpose that informs, illuminates, and heals.

KNIGHT of SWORDS.

Knight of Pentacles: Element of earth; manifestation; triumph through "working with natural God-given talents." Real tangible possessions and powers, and the successful handling of them, including the fair consideration of the needs and wants of others. Challenge of charity toward self and others; kindness, compassion.

KNIGHT of PENTACLES

Position 5. The Page

The Page represents the type of action needed for spirit to reach matter. In other words, what to do to attain the goal or desired outcome of the question asked. He describes the future and what will come to pass. Pages are the elemental work—i.e., ritual and practices actually "working with" the four elements of fire, water, air, and earth. The placement and card define the aspect of self to develop, what you should do.

Page of Wands: Will. Develop clarity of what your authentic will desires. Follow the feelings, inspirations, and aspirations indicated by intensification and growth of your true passion. Indicates manifestation of a matter that is dear to the personal self and true nature. Follow through on real desires.

Reversed: Inability to clarify what is real or authentic; remedy is in upright interpretation, put the true self first.

Page of Cups: Flow. Manifestation of unconscious elements through psychic means, dreams, or impressions. Develop meditative, intuitive, and imaginative skills to interact with the potentials held in the unconscious, and the life will become inspired and soulful. Flow with and heed dreams and meditative content; follow your intuition. Nurture self. Manifestation of the power of love; emotional understanding.

Reversed: Inability to allow development of relationship with above-mentioned traits.

Page of Swords: Action based on messages of synchronicity; be open to occurrences of a symbolic or coincidental nature and take time to analyze their content. Manifestation of important communication or conversation that may point to a surprising direction;

be flexible and adaptable with your attitude and viewpoints. Unknown factors may surface and change the scenario or confirm suspicions. Maintain willingness to adjust perspective; reveals new thinking on a matter that will help determine choices and actions. Manifestation of decision-making, discrimination, ordering, and categorizing. Learning.

PAGE OF SWORDS.

Reversed: Same as upright.

PAGE OF PENTACLES

Page of Pentacles: Manifestation of matter of a practical, realistic nature—i.e., money, job, education; a project with a purpose. Action that results in helpful knowledge, health, the gathering and analysis of information. Practice grounding techniques and connecting fully to your body and external environment. This often opens up unrevealed instincts and tremendous reservoirs of wisdom, intuition, and connection to important realizations through experiences and feelings. Also aspects of the self being "worked" on, including bodywork; spiritual practices involving movement, dance, yoga, walks, etc., are very empowering. Do these activities with a self-observant mind. Self-respect and self-worth are strongly felt and communicated as an established strength and will be responded to in kind. Formation, sustenance, commitment. Build, secure, establish, maintain.

Reversed: Inability to ground and feel comfortable and strong within the real, tangible world. Problems being open-minded, in the "here and now," and fully establishing a life force that embraces the earthly life, tendency toward wasting one's time, talent, and resources. Difficulty accepting the body with its blessings and challenges. Need to practice grounding techniques and taking constructive action rather than living in one's mind.

SAMPLE READING

This reading was cast for a woman named Jo-Ann. She had just returned from a visit with her accountant and felt frustrated and dismayed at her inability to move her finances into full prosperity. Tired of being in a surviving, not thriving, economic state, Jo-Ann asked the cards for guidance from the Whole Self spread, hoping to attain new information to work with for solving her problem.

4

2

1

3

5

Position 1   The Ace of Swords
Position 2   King of Pentacles
Position 3   Queen of Cups
Position 4   Knight of Pentacles
Position 5   Page of Pentacles

Overall observations immediately point to the presence of three Pentacle cards, indicative that, indeed, the cards are revealing monetary solutions. The suit of Wands is absent, therefore a message about courage and bravery is essential to understanding the interpretation.

Position 1

The Ace of Swords reveals the spiritual solution, lesson, and healing agent involved with the inquiry. The interpretation of lessons and solutions involving integrity, honesty, and being fair to one's self felt powerful to Jo-Ann. She admitted that, although her business made her a modest and adequate income, her real avocation was currently marginalized due to immediate economic needs. She felt out of integrity because her true vocation wasn't fully embraced. Jo-Ann wasn't being fair to herself or her talents, a gift from God (the Pentacles interpretation of charity). She knew she had strength acquired through adversity, and the card was pointing to this asset to remind her and validate her experiences. When a card comments on something already integrated, it often does so to serve as a foundation of success on which to build new strengths. The message was clear; she indeed was strong enough to pursue her true career path by using a constructive attitude and discipline.

Position 2

The King of Pentacles in this placement is read as the ego strengths, the personality that the Seeker uses to move through daily life. The King of Pentacles indicated that Jo-Ann was regarded as good at earning and saving money by herself and with others. Jo-Ann confirmed that her life had many riches in possessions, living standard, and property. She was viewed as rich in talents. Indeed, she was endowed with numerous gifts and aptitudes. The interpretation of such a positive affluent persona gave her confidence. Ironically, she perceived herself as a well-off individual—more than her bank account could attest to. I encouraged her to keep this personal identity, as it will serve to attract the money she desires. The message of being charitable toward herself also rang true, because she was being hard on herself.

Position 3

The Queen of Cups in this position represents who Jo-Ann is unconsciously, and the power she can realize and utilize. The Queen of Cups describes an unconscious power source that is intuitive, creative, and connected to the flow of universal inspiration. The more she embraces her depth, the more clearly the muse will direct her and the deeper her connection with faith will become. I advised her to devote herself to what brings her joy and use it for motivation.

The Queen of Cups receives powerful guidance from intuitive messages such as a reading, meditation, or, in this case, a dream. Subsequent to the reading, Jo-Ann had a dream that revealed an emotionally toxic past that related to her question. Because the Queen and the spread placement represent unrealized or only partially understood power sources, this dream was instrumental for her. It showed a connection between her monetary situation and the past that she had ignored. She was then able to use the Justice card meditation (see page 182) to sever the ties that bound her to her past. (The reading's message doesn't stop when the session ends; it continues to offer guidance in the following days, because the soul and subconscious have been triggered to offer insight.) Her choice to meditate on the dream demonstrates a Cups power.

Position 4

The Knight of Pentacles indicates the triumph and challenge to work with her natural God-given talents. With this suit, the magic is in the making. In other words, once you are involved in the doing process, rather than just thinking or dreaming, the necessary ingredients will present themselves. I advised Jo-Ann (remember that Wands are absent) to involve herself simply and courageously, but in tangible ways, with the avocation she'd marginalized and to have the faith (the Cups theme) that prosperity and economic abundance would come to her.

Position 5

The Page of Pentacles in this placement represents the action to take to create empowerment. It describes the future and the qualities needed for spirit to reach form. The Page of Pentacles advises taking practical steps toward a goal. Gather pertinent information and helpful knowledge. Pay attention to spiritual body practices, for, when you work with the body, the idea is that physical action, whether ritual, ceremony, or intentional doing, yields tangible results. The Page of Pentacles was predicting that Jo-Ann would become knowledgeable and informed about her new avocation, including the monetary aspect of it. It would materialize; she would become immersed in her chosen vocation through a realistic knowledge-based plan of action. With the money-making know-how in place, she'd be able to fulfill her goal of manifestation of abundance in her chosen profession.

Once the fivefold self is realized, you can harmonize the parts of the reading into a new way of self-understanding. Creative problem-resolution culled from within your own nature is a wonderful way to unfold and develop your potentials. The Whole Self reading provides guidance founded on the theme of personal responsibility blended with a deepened awareness of your spiritual gifts, lessons, and resources for empowerment and real evolution that I believe the cards can reveal.

• 6 •

THE FOUR SEASONS
SPREAD

The Four Seasons spread is used four times a year on the day of the equinoxes of autumn and spring, and the solstices of summer and winter. These days are powerful and a good time to get a glimpse into the season ahead. This is a predictive spread; it uses timing based on the seasons, Moon cycles, and the numbers of the cards.

THE LAYOUT

Start by separating your cards into the fours suits, Ace through King, and the Major Arcana. You will have five piles. Next, shuffle each pile separately, while asking the cards for a forecast for the specific season. After the shuffling is finished, place the piles in front of you and locate the Wands pile. Fan them, facedown. Some cards will be upright and some reversed. Pass your left hand, or your receiving hand (this will be the one where you feel energy), over the cards until one seems to attract you. You may feel an energy wave being emitted or a magnetic pull or tug from the card. Place this card in Position 1 in the diagram shown on page 100, facedown. Repeat the fanning and card-selection process, placing the Cups card in Position 2, the Swords card in Position 3, and the Pentacles card in Position 4, all facedown. Finish by

The Four Seasons Spread

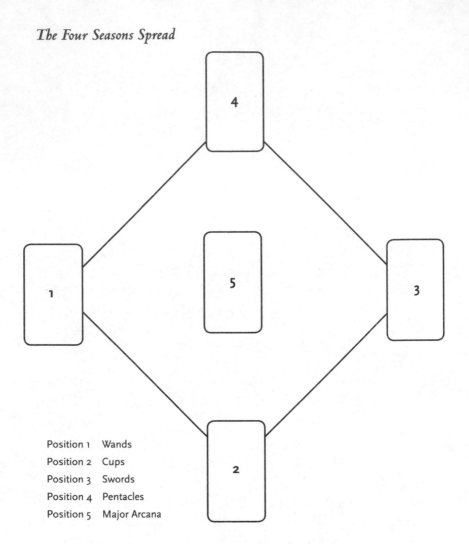

Position 1   Wands
Position 2   Cups
Position 3   Swords
Position 4   Pentacles
Position 5   Major Arcana

fanning the Major Arcana and choosing one to place in the center of the diamond diagram.

Begin the reading by turning over the Major Arcana. This is the spiritual theme, power, and lesson that governs the season.

Turn over the card in Position I—the Wands card. This is a message regarding your energy and how you will spend it during the season. The Wands card will reveal your genuine feelings, especially related to your will, enthusiasm, desires, wants, and what is stirring within you. For example, the card may indicate whether you will feel like exploring (Two of Wands), feel burned-out or overburdened (Ten of Wands), or feel inspired to take the lead (Six of Wands). It is important to honor and respond to these natural promptings bravely, since they are authentic and connect you with your inner self. Use courage and fortitude when addressing how to handle these desires.

The card in Position 2 is the Cups card. Emotional conditions, loved ones, and your romantic relationship and feelings are revealed in this placement. Intuitive insights or messages from various sources, such as a Tarot reading, dream, or psychic prompting can be read here. For example, if the Page of Cups reversed appears, this indicates a lack of faith and important dreams and psychic promptings that are unheeded or not remembered. Conversely, if the Four of Cups presented itself an important dream would be remembered and contemplated.

Your intuition will respond to the correct interpretation of this card. This placement is particularly useful for individuals who find connecting to their intuition a challenge. Read the card, keeping in mind the virtues of love and faith affiliated with the Cups suit.

The card in Position 3 is the Swords card. This will indicate your intelligence, attitude, and mental focus for the season. Swords indicate how you are thinking, what is being thought about, and conscious awareness of how you perceive your world. If you pick a destructive or struggling card (e.g., Nine of Swords, Ace of Swords reversed), take a step back and observe the integrity, motivation, and thinking behind your actions. The card is asking you to learn from your thoughts and behavioral patterns. Review how your beliefs and words contribute to disharmony and conflict. Ask yourself if this is the best and healthiest choice for you to make in light of the Swords meaning of truth.

The virtue of justice and the various swords of power listed in the suit interpretation section on page 251 will help you define the best way to prepare your intellect for the season. Positive cards will indicate constructive thinking, learning, and consciousness-raising, whereas negative cards will show unjust destructive thinking in need of revision and adjustment.

Now turn over the card in Position 4—a Pentacle. This is a message about Pentacle matters—labors of love, reality, real occurrences, finances, health, practical matters, work, job, security, or possessions. Upright cards generally indicate stability and security, whereas reversed are indicative of struggle and instability. Interpret this card using the virtue of charity expressed through giving and development of the talents described by the card.

You now have four predictions for the three-month season, as well as a spiritual power to meditate on. Now apply the timing factors to experiment with predictive timing. For example, autumn begins when the Sun enters the zodiacal sign of Libra. Check your astrological calendar or Web site for the dates when the Moon will be in Libra for the following three months. These dates (there will be two days in each month) may be turning points when the cards' prediction occurs. Repeat the process when you recast the reading for the following seasons. Winter predictions may happen during the Moon sign of Capricorn; spring may occur in Moon in Aries; summer predictions may occur in Moon in Cancer. Each season will have two days when the Moon sign matches the equinox or solstice sign of the season, and they can be marked on the calendar along with the New and Full Moon. These may also be days on which events come to pass.

Another way to experiment with timing is to use the cards' numbers to predict weeks. For example, the event foreshadowed by the Six of Cups will happen six weeks into the season. Yet another option is to add up the entire set of numbers and then add the resulting two digits. This reduces the reading to one final number that may predict the week when events will happen.

Sample Reading

Robert cast a reading for the winter season on the winter solstice. He observed that day happened to mark a Full Moon, then added another timing factor. He noted when the other months' Full Moons occurred and factored that into the timing of the events the cards forecast. If you have a New Moon on the day of your reading, watch the New Moons in the upcoming months for predictions to come to pass.

The reading laid out like this:

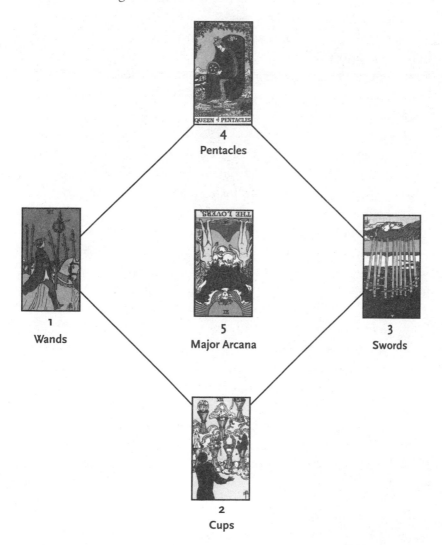

4
Pentacles

1
Wands

5
Major Arcana

3
Swords

2
Cups

Position 1   Six of Wands
Position 2   Seven of Cups
Position 3   Ten of Swords reversed
Position 4   Queen of Pentacles
Position 5   The Lovers reversed

I knew I had my interpretive work cut out for me when I saw The Lovers reversed. The card revealed a lack of intimacy, relationship problems, poor communication, and interference from others in important partnerships. I scanned the other cards and saw the Queen of Pentacles and the Seven of Cups. Because of The Lovers and the Queen of Pentacles, I felt that the winter season would be centered on relationship and romantic matters. The upright meaning of healing associated with The Lovers was obviously the underlying theme of the season. However, the Arcanum's reversal suggested Robert was unconscious about the prospect or the possibility of healing his emotional life. With the Ten of Swords reversed, suggesting a new consciousness and the dawn of a fresh perspective in the Swords position, I felt Robert was just beginning to see the light of a better day. I felt he intuited hope and was seeking it subconsciously.

The cards suggested that a physical (not imagined or idealized) woman with a charitable nature (Queen of Pentacles) would be in his life during the winter. He said he was alone, having ended a companionship with a woman over a year ago. I told him that I thought the ending had gone poorly and that there was difficulty in communication, trouble with intimacy, and possible interference from another source. He confided that she was married and simply had ended the affair, to his disappointment.

I chose to forecast a new woman in his life, but wondered if he'd be ready for her (The Lovers reversed). The emotional tone of the reading naturally caused me to look at the Cups card he'd chosen. The Seven of Cups is a challenging card. It asks the Seeker to decipher what is truly of heartfelt value. The indications were uncertainty—maybe he wanted fame, or wealth, or to be with a beloved, and maybe not. But difficulty making choices with genuine integrity is another meaning of The Lovers reversed. A lesson concerning his ambivalence in keeping new love at arms' length and a willingness to be intimate was indicated.

Perhaps the attitude toward the events of the season (The Swords position) would help me with a healing message for Robert. The Ten of Swords was reversed; I could use that to say that his wounds from the past were healing (The Lovers' theme was repeating) and that a new day was dawning. His thinking would be turning toward fresh beginnings and a more optimistic viewpoint about life.

Looking at his Wand card, we have the Six of Wands, indicating that his natural leadership ability would be recognized and honored. His well-balanced efforts would yield rewarding results. This also told me that he was naturally a brave soul with effective, natural people skills.

The final analysis of the season took me back to the Queen of Pentacles. I told him he would meet a gracious, down-to-earth woman. They would share similar values and appreciate each other's gifts and aptitudes. The opportunity to heal the emotional past would be given to him, and he would succeed by allowing intimacy—a key aspect of The Lovers, where the individuals reveal their hearts and souls to each other. He said he'd always wanted to be loved for himself, but didn't realize that, in order to have that happen, he had to allow it and be comfortable with heartfelt communication from others toward him. He was expressing his feelings honestly during the reading. I pointed this out to him, mentioning that he could be sincere with himself and others too, just as we were doing at that moment.

I felt the new woman would be similar in character to Robert and that she would be emotionally mature and help his own maturation. Healing would come in the form of a new love for Robert. He will use his successful people skills (Six of Wands) and new optimistic attitude (Ten of Swords reversed) to turn The Lovers upright and heal. This would happen in approximately six to ten weeks (I used the sixes from The Lovers and Six of Wands and the other cards indicated seven and ten). The dates of the Full Moon were also noted for events to unfold.

NEW MEANINGS
& MEDITATIONS
FOR THE
MAJOR ARCANA

In Part Three, we'll examine the essence of the Tarot. Symbolism, the Infinite Intelligence, and the Higher Self in relationship to the trump cards are explained. The value in cultivating a relationship with these soul qualities is that they serve as protectors as well as guides for your spiritual development and journey.

· 7 ·

THE MAJOR ARCANA, 0–7

The series of Major Arcana from 0-7 show pure archetypal energies:

> 0: Spirit—The Fool
> 1: The Self—The Magician
> 2: The Soul—The High Priestess
> 3: Creation—The Empress
> 4: Manifested Mastery—The Emperor
> 5: Spiritual Knowledge—The Hierophant
> 6: Healing Love—The Lovers
> 7: The Hero—The Chariot.

When they appear in a layout, focus your interpretation on the spiritual power represented. When reversed, utilize the upright meaning as the key quality needed for guidance. The 0–7 Majors are highly powerful life transformers and spiritual initiators when meditated upon, especially sequentially.

THE ESSENCE OF THE TAROT

What is the spiritual essence of Tarot? The essence or foundation of the Tarot is Divine Mind and recognized by the Higher Self. Just like other systems of occult knowledge, Tarot is a channel and representation of metaphysical energy and principles from the Higher Mind or super-conscious, also known as Infinite Intelligence.

The Higher Mind feels peaceful, spiritual, and clear; it thinks at you. Its thought always contains help, insight, and guidance. It is always in communication with you, and it already exists within your soul. The powers and soul lessons contained within it interact with your conscious and subconscious mind through visions, dreams, and metaphysics—through readings, meditation, and psychic messages. Spirits, angels, "aha" moments or epiphanies, genius, miracles, or healings, come from the Higher Mind. Your personal experience of these aspects of the Higher Mind is depicted in The Lovers, where the card's characters perceive an emissary from the divine plane through their spiritual intuition of Higher Self. This capacity is called "discernment of the spirit."

This contact occurs through a radiating energy force, telepathy, and information being sent to you. An energy shift occurs within you that feels clear and aligned. This heightened sensitivity may be accompanied by an inner knowing, as wisdom through psychic awareness or heartfelt knowing. This is called direct cognition of the spirit. The Hermit represents this quality.

You can connect with the Higher Mind using meditation and the Tarot. Meditation awakens the dormant spiritual essence in your personal Higher Mind and stimulates the divine nature held in the occult heart. The twenty-two Major Arcana, or trumps (also known as "books" or "keys"), actually depict the dynamics of how the powers of the soul and spirit function. They also portray the lesson through symbolism.

Symbols are awakeners, transformers, and a source of communication from the spiritual dimension. They serve as contact points for the Divine archetypal energy. The archetypes of the Tarot's Major Arcana are specialized frequencies from the Infinite Intelligence.

Those who are drawn to the Tarot have an affinity with symbolism. It is through interaction with symbols that you transform yourself because of the powerful archetypes and energies within them. They are already in relationship to you; you simply need to become conscious of them. There are many way to accomplish this purpose—for example, meditation, contemplation, invocation, using affirmation, and journaling.

When you perform readings for yourself and focus on the message of the cards, you activate the transformative qualities of the cards' symbols. When you interpret a reading, look at the Major Arcana and dominant suit, and ask yourself how you can facilitate a physical participation by expressing or making something out of the symbols presented there.

There are many ways to concretize the magical power of symbols:

Create a work of art—through music, dance, painting, collage, scrapbooking, or literature.

Pursue scholarly research—write a book or make a film.

Make an altar, create a ceremony.

Cultivate a garden or landscape; create floral arrangements.

Design clothing or wear the colors of an archetype.

Make jewelry, study gemology, pursue crafts.

Design original architecture or interior decoration; visit locations that reflect the symbols.

Photograph subjects that capture the archetype and symbol, then create an album to capture and share the images with others.

The idea is to blend the symbols with a life skill in which you are adept, or that you enjoy or want to master—all the while being mindful of the archetype behind the subject of your craft. When you participate in this way, the universe will respond by bringing you personal and life transformation. You cannot control how and when this transformation will occur. It is usually spontaneous, immediate, and has long-term effects. You can only receive and respond to what you are given. In this way, you collaborate with the Divine Mind and, in essence, experience the joyous masterful expression of Spirit in matter represented by The World trump.

Following are some examples of participation with a symbol to facilitate transformation:

 Design and plant a garden using red and white flowers, lilies and roses (The Magician or The Hierophant).

 Visit a sacred mountain and climb to the top (The Hermit).

 Overhaul or design a motorcycle, car, or other vehicle; run a race or marathon, or build other athletic skills (The Chariot).

 Train a pet (Strength).

 Visit a sacred location with a special spiritual attribute— the Wonders of the World, the rain forests; explore environmental causes (The World).

 Try parasailing, skydiving, or hot-air ballooning (The Fool).

 Visit ancient spiritual sites—temple ruins, cathedrals (The High Priestess).

Create a special garden or garden area with the spiritual design elements of circle or triangle, special trees, and attention to sunlight (The Lovers, The Empress, The Sun).

Participate in medieval, Renaissance, and military reenactments (The Emperor, the Court cards).

 Attend a school, conference, or other study program (The Hierophant).

 Travel for educational reasons (Wheel of Fortune).

Help others through charitable, political, and social activism (Justice, The Star).

 Attend a spiritual retreat (The Hanged Man).

Attend a celebration or feast for the dead (Death).

Get involved with angelology
(Temperance, The Lovers, The Hermit, and Judgement).

Demolish something; participate in a demolition derby
(The Tower).

Find a dark corner that needs light and install a light fixture, or light a candle in a dark place
(The Hermit).

Grow sunflowers; enjoy raising children
(The Sun).

Spend an evening outdoors under the Full Moon or in the wilds of nature at night (The Moon).

Research your family genealogy (Judgement).

The four Tarot suits portray how the archetypal essences are expressed in human nature (the Court cards) and in everyday life (the Minor Arcana Aces through Tens.)

Wands represent dedication of energy and will to an authentic purpose. This evokes and imparts courage.

Cups are expressed through the ability to merge with the spiritual powers, becoming a channel for their expression. This requires and instills faith.

Swords display the Higher Mind by consciousness-raising through meditation and positive thought that penetrates into the realm of genius, inspiration, guidance, and intuition, then translates the information, sharing it with the world. Integrity and constructive use of thought is a Sword-suit power.

Pentacles express the Infinite Intelligence through the "earthing or grounding" of energy in the physical body. You center the energy within you using breathing practices, yoga, conscious action, and ritual. Containment is the essence. The Pentacles realm is one of laboring lovingly to make tangible things happen and tending to the creation. When you want to produce real concrete change, meditate on this suit.

BEGINNING YOUR JOURNEY

This exercise is designed to give you a conscious connection with each archetype, its symbol, and its divine message as you start to learn about the Major Arcana. It will give you a clear theme for this particular time in your life. You can also use it to guide you to future and even past events by simply repeating the instructions and participating in the practice.

Separate your deck into the four Minor Arcana Aces and the Major Arcana. Shuffle the Major Arcana cards, then fan them facedown. Ask the cards to reveal the spiritual energy that is currently working with you, or ask which spiritual lesson and power will be your theme as you read this book. Pass your hand over the cards until one feels as if it should be chosen. Place the card facedown in front of you.

Now repeat the procedure with Minor Arcana Aces. This will show you how best to express the quintessence of the Major Arcana card in your daily life through the virtues of the suit meanings.

Date:_____

Major Arcanum chosen: _____

Ace chosen: _____

Read the card descriptions, interpretations, questions, affirmations, and quotes given below, as well as the meditation for the chosen Major Arcanum. Take time to perform the meditation and write down your experiences, as well as their aftermath. Relate the suit of the Ace chosen and its virtue meaning (Wands, courage; Cups, faith; Swords, justice; Pentacles, charity) to the Major Arcanum.

For example, assume The Moon was chosen for the Major card and the Ace of Wands for the Minor card. The Moon relates to the unconscious, the psychic, and the maternal. The meditation involves the purification of the psychic energy field. The Ace of Wands indicates that the courage needed to perform the meditation and to face what may be encountered. Perhaps the quality of bravery is locked in the unconscious and, by working with the affirmations or questions of the Moon card, a new connection can be made to this quality. Fortitude to maintain a strong connection to the psychic realms and communicate their messages is an equally valid analysis. The idea is that all of the interpretations are useful and applicable, as well as the new ones that may result from them.

As you work with or interact with the two cards, new ideas will form about what you can do to collaborate with the archetypes and symbols. In this example, spending a night outdoors under the Moon may help with a lesson in courage.

When you awaken to and interact with divine Tarot energies, the effects are empowering. Refer back to the information often, for there are many aspects to these soul lessons. Record your initial impressions in a Tarot journal. This is a special notebook for writing your readings, interpretations, thoughts, revelations, and messages. Continue to write in the journal as you read this book. Refer back to this original card pull of Ace and Major Arcanum, and ponder its significance in light of your ever-unfolding Tarot journey.

The Major Arcana have practical interpretations you can use when reading. Special spiritual descriptions that highlight the occult essence of the card provide fresh insight. The meditations will give you a deepened understanding of the metaphysical principles they represent. Ask yourself the soul-based questions given and use the affirmations. Then perform the meditation practices given to open your consciousness to a new level of spiritual awareness through the amazing power of the Tarot.

THE FOOL

If the Fool would persist in his folly he would become wise.
(WILLIAM BLAKE)

The Fool steps out of the heavens and into creation through his desire to be known. The mystical belief in the presence of the divine light concealed within human nature is represented by this great Arcanum. In truth, we are the possessors of the greatest spiritual treasure, and we can experience it directly in the here and now. The divine spark of the inner light is the flame of cosmic love that beats within all of our hearts. It initiates and fuels The Fool's journey toward the experiences that will provide the knowledge and understanding of his spiritual nature.

Interpretation

A new life cycle begins. Birth and brilliance. A big risk yields big rewards. An evolutionary choice prompted by the soul's wisdom. Autonomy. A happy surprise. Destiny knocks.

The Fool represents your Higher Self's involvement with your inquiry, an important birth of soul potential and movement toward its expression is indicated when it appears in a reading. The journey inward to reclaim your soul or the journey outward to manifest your soul's potential, whichever constitutes a new direction. The birth of new or enhanced character strengths like faith, courage, self-confidence, dedication, and self-esteem open the door to a cycle of joy and fulfillment. Trust in the universe and you may attain more than you ever dreamed possible.

The Fool denotes authentic life progression based on innocence, trust, truth, faith, and the purity of the genuine, spiritual heart. The divine spark intensifies through the expression of your heartfelt individuality. If your choice or opportunity reflects what God or divinity would want for you, then it is a wise desire worth visioning and following.

The Fool is powered by the super-conscious or Infinite Intelligence. The foliage that appears on his tunic represents the seeds of the gifts of the Spirit. These gifts were once known as the "gifts of faith" and include prophecy, healing powers, and divination. They represent your personal genius and your soul purpose.

Embarking upon a new opportunity toward unfoldment yields very positive results. The Fool's joyful expectation signifies positivity. Be open to new adventures in life. Allow yourself to find your own path and unfold your unique truth.

When faced with a choice, ask, "Would Divinity want this for me?" Proceed if the answer is yes, knowing that you are incarnated to learn joyful and challenging lessons.

Reversed meaning: The Fool reversed is akin to a stop sign; do not proceed until you have more information. Your judgment is untrustworthy, as are the circumstances involved in the question. Mistakes. Confusion regarding who you really are, how you truly feel in the matter; lack of clarity, fearfulness. Inability to trust the intuition that goads you toward knowing your authentic self and developing character strengths. You need more soul-searching; wait to make choices; an imbalance needs to be rectified first.

Questions to Consider

- How do I feel about taking a leap of faith? What were the results of previous leaps of faith? What have I learned and need to integrate and refine?

- Does this step represent aspirations and hopes for my future well-being? Am I about to leap headlong into something that simply recreates a past pattern of detriment (The Fool reversed)?

- Does spiritual aspiration govern my physical, mental, and emotional life?

- Does this involvement represent unfoldment of my potentials?

- What am I on the edge of? Discovering something about myself, my desires and potentials? What am I on the brink of? New expanded awareness, starting something new? Putting the pieces of something together?

- If I look deep inside myself, what will I discover?

- What am I about to externalize?

- Who am I?

Affirmations

I am now in full awareness of who I really am.

I choose faith.

I can.

The universe protects me completely. I trust in its flow to bring me more than I ever dreamed possible.

I am in perfect alignment with the energy and harmony of the universe.

I joyfully open my heart, life, and soul to unfolding the seeds of the gifts of the Spirit within me.

The limitless Infinite Intelligence is the essence and light within me.

I open myself to my limitless source and potential.

Meditation

The Fool card introduces the two essential meditation qualities of light and breath. Breathing techniques, especially those of yoga's *pranayama*, correspond to it. Divinity breathes out when you breathe in; it breathes in when you breathe out. All life experience starts with the breath and the occult principle of *pranayama*. We'll explore these spiritual breathing techniques in this section.

Use this card in meditation and visualization to overcome fearfulness about making a fool of yourself and to determine whether your choice is foolish or wise. Ask for the white light of clarity and truth to shine upon your situation from all angles. Pure light is the child of divine thought, which becomes the knowledge of certainty in The Sun card. Note the relationship between The Sun and The Fool.

Meditate upon The Fool to attract new potentials, fresh starts, and limitless potential. He brings joy and optimism, and relieves negativity. He also attracts positive transformative conditions.

Two meditation techniques that can be applied to the entire Tarot are symbolized in this great arcanum. The card begins the Major Arcana series and therefore contains the practices for the soul's journey toward an awareness of its spiritual nature.

The White Light of Alignment and Protection and the Occult Heart are the two techniques that open the soul and provide safe passage. These simple exercises involve the mind, body, and spirit. They are fundamental for easy and successful experiences in meditation.

The White Light of Alignment and Protection breathing exercise provides serenity and opens the channel to the Higher Mind, the source of true meditation. The Occult Heart technique is a method for connecting with a symbol, from the Tarot or from another source. The practice develops an activation of a new connection to the super-conscious and stimulates the spark of your spiritual nature. Once ignited and kindled, it will become your methodology for understanding all the Tarot cards.

Learning the techniques attributed to The Fool will provide the foundation and protection for your spiritual sojourn. The purpose of meditating on The Fool is to attract new potentials, fresh starts, limitless possibilities, and optimum thinking. When you invite The Fool's energy into your life, beneficial ideas and perceptions will naturally pop up or be presented to you through synchronistic, serendipitous events. Optimism and a trustworthy positive change of heart can also occur. When this happens, you know that your meditation has been effective.

An oval of white light encompasses The Fool in many versions of the card. This is known as the "cosmic egg" of all potential; it is also a shielding tool. Light is a manifestation of the divine knowledge. When Divinity appears to the mind of the mystic, it is pure, uncontaminated light. Your soul is "lighter" than your physical body; it appears as light and encourages you to "be" light of heart and spirit, as The Fool illustrates.

When you embark on any new journey, including a spiritual one, you must know how to invoke protection and ensure safe passage. This White Light technique can be used for all protection-oriented situations.

The White Light of Alignment and Protection

Prana means "breath"; *yama* means "pause." *Pranayama* consists of exhalation, suspension, and inhalation. The practice of this breathing technique regulates the breath and is a fundamental step toward enlightenment. Those who perform these practices are regarded as treading the path of light.

Pranayama is said to burn up karma from other lifetimes and the current incarnation. It frees the mind from all illusion and awakens spiritual energy; it refines and accelerates growth. Calmness and mental powers are attained through it, as are weight reduction and control over the sympathetic nervous system.

This is the breathing technique used in conjunction with all of our meditative exercises in this volume. Move your breath from the diaphragm or the solar plexus area gently. Breathe in to a slow count of four; hold for a count of four; breathe out for a slow count of four. This is a calming breath technique. Inhale, hold, then exhale in a rhythmic count to the fullest of your capacity, making sure that you use the same count on your inhalations as you do for your suspension (or hold) and exhalation. You can increase this count gradually until you reach sixteen. Practice this breathing with your mouth closed; do it for twenty-four minutes per day, or fifteen minutes in the morning and evening.

Start by taking four pranayama-style or deep cleansing breaths. Sense, visualize, or become aware of the crown of your head, then feel it becoming warm and soft while breathing.

Experience a white light warmly and gently sprouting out of the top of your head. Radiate, beam, or channel a ray of the light down to the space below the soles of your feet, then move the light back up to your crown. Repeat until you have covered all sides of your body. Bask in the sealed, white-light protection, then allow it to become larger and penetrate you, so that you stand completely protected as if you were the yoke of an egg—the cosmic egg.

This practice aligns you with your spiritual core in whatever way required. If you perform this exercise daily, it will bring serenity and balance. The protection it provides is effective with people, nations, the world, cars, kids, pets, and residences.

The Occult Heart

This is a basic meditation technique for all symbols and Arcana. The Occult Heart meditation is an Eastern practice that involves taking the symbol or deity into your heart space—i.e., your heart chakra—through sensing or imaging its presence channeled on a ray of light that beams into the heart area within you. Perform this meditation after relaxing your body and after performing at least four rounds of pranayama breathing.

You can use this technique throughout your journey into mysticism. It especially highlights the spiritual qualities of symbolism. The character in the Four of Cups illustrates this procedure. He sits in a meditative lotus position, or cross-legged, and contemplates the vision of a chalice held parallel to his heart and head.

Begin by choosing a Tarot card or symbol you wish to understand or activate in anticipation of the potential becoming tangible. For example, if you desire to delve more deeply into your metaphysical, prophetic powers, visualize The High Priestess; if you want to communicate with your Spiritual Guide, use The Hermit; if you want to make something tangible (money, job, etc.), work with the Ace of Pentacles.

Visualize or sense the symbol or card hovering directly outside your heart, as illustrated in the Four of Cups. Continue the

breathing technique as you imagine a ray of light or an energy field emanating from the symbol visualized at your heart, but outside it. Now, on your inhalation, bring the image into your heart. Hold it there, then breathe it out. Repeat two or more times. This stimulates an awakening of the secrets that are hidden in the occult aspect of your heart and soul. The practice is especially recommended for the Tarot symbols to activate their transformative archetypal powers.

Each breathing cycle will bring new responses from the symbol. Let the symbol show you what it wants to reveal. Your super-conscious connection to your Higher Self will give you an insight, a vision of the past or future, an unrealized viewpoint, spiritual inner guidance, or soul awareness. This may come in the form of a memory, a perception, an "aha" moment, a flash of perception, a sensation with information, or through hearing words that state an important message. Let it travel inside you, becoming very large or changing dimension as it sees fit. Note and record the change, but do not control it. Notice how it appears as it moves out of you.

The power of the symbol will manifest as required by your spiritual nature. For example, you may choose a symbol with a specific purpose in mind. As the practice unfolds, the symbol will evolve, bringing a different gift, revealing a surprising agenda of its own. The hallmark of a real meditative experience is precisely this aspect—it should reveal something new, wise, and illuminating.

Note the results in the forms of images, external responses from other people, situations you attract, and your thoughts, dreams, and realizations during the following days. The outcome of the meditation will fulfill The Fool's mandate for you to know your spiritual nature.

THE MAGICIAN

Nature brings to light nothing that is perfect, but man must perfect it. This perfection is called alchimia. An alchemist is the baker when he bakes bread, the viniculturist when he makes wine, the weaver when he makes cloth.
(PARACELSUS, *PARAGRANUM*)

The Magician trump has evolved over the past few centuries. Gone are the earlier versions of a juggler, con man, conjurer, and unreliable trickster. Now he appears magically transformed into The Alchemist, dedicated to the cultivation of the spiritual aspect of our human desires, an activity known as the initiate's "Great Work." The Arcanum's pictorial progression is a fitting metaphor for the transformation of our desires from lower to higher.

The Magician represents humankind as mediator between nature and the cosmos. Only humans have the special capacity of consciousness-raising and personality evolution. Their position is unique because they possess the attributes of creativity, choice, and self-awareness through the gift of the conscious mind.

Interpretation

The power of concentration. That toward which you dedicate yourself will become your life. The creative principle; you are your creations. Imaginative ideas. Initiative, invention, genius, and entrepreneurship.

The personal will dedicated toward great aspiration. The beginning and development of a meaningful endeavor. Ideas that are being implemented; projects worked on with diligence, devotion, and continuity. Discipline, organization, and focus; one thing at a time. Discipleship. Character building; focus on strengthening, balancing, and spiritualization of heart, mind, and body.

You are your creations and the center of your universe. You have been gifted with a conscious mind and ego; use them to the highest good. Become a servant of the light. Keep this in mind, first and foremost, and all will be added unto you.

True magic arises when you choose the spiritual value and purpose of your intention—in other words, when you evolve an ambition into an aspiration. Cultivate the purest, most ideal form of that which you desire (do not omit your desires), then plant the seed. If you include the open heart (Cups), fortitude and will to do good (Wands), clear and balanced mind and action (Swords), and disciplined body productively tending to a labor of love (Pentacles), your desire will grow and blossom.

Reversed meaning: Living too much in the mind, intellectual dialogues. Escaping into thoughts and reflecting on life rather than living life-making choices and engaging in productive activity. Immaturity, problems with responsibility; lack of introspection, negative attitude toward life. Manipulation and tricky sleights of hand; an untrustworthy situation.

Questions to Consider

- Where are my attention and imagination focused? How does this serve me?

- What needs organization and discipline in my life? In me?

- Am I serious about my devotion to my personal evolution?

- What are my true intentions?

- What am I really here to do?

- What do I sincerely wish to accomplish?

- Do I allow myself the energy, will, and time to achieve what I desire?

- Do I keep an open heart and allow myself to receive and transmit the power of love, creativity, and spirituality?

- How do I channel my energy? Is it blocked or does it flow freely toward my intention?

- Do my actions mirror my intentions?

Affirmations

I am that I am.

As above, so below.

That which is above is as that which is below and that which is below is as that which is above.

Of myself, I am nothing; I do the will of the one who sent me.

Meditation

The Magician meditation is a guided visualization. You may wish to have it read to you or to record it and play it back to yourself. Or simply refer to it as you proceed through the visualization. This technique applies to all of the Tarot exercises in this volume.

The Magician card is numbered one. The inference of placing yourself in the number one position as the "center" of your own life is primary for spiritual growth. The tools you utilize to fulfill The Magician's mandate to "Know thyself" are symbolized by the four implements of the Tarot suits placed before him. The secret is that each of us has a special Wand, Cup, Sword, and Pentacle that exist on the astral or etheric plane of the soul.

The purpose of the Magician meditation is to see, interact with, and integrate these four magical implements. Once perceived and activated, the tools then become talismans, symbols, and touchstones for the accomplishment of your "Great Work."

Discovering Your Higher Self

Place The Magician in front of you and begin with deep breathing and relaxation. Make sure you will have ample time for this meditation. As with all the practices, a journal, notebook, pen, candle, and appropriate music enhance the experience.

Imagine, visualize, or sense yourself standing among roses. They form a bower above you and grow at your feet. Now smell the scent of roses. Another perfume fills the air. Note what images and responses come to mind. It is the scent of lilies and now you see their presence intermingled with the roses. Fill your senses of sight and smell with these beautiful flowers. Understand that they represent essence—the highest, finest, most spiritual offering from the vegetable world. Touch the petals. Embrace them. Examine them.

Next, you discover a wooden table. Four tools are placed on it, and behind it stands The Magician himself. Behold his grandeur; feel his presence. Is he shimmering? Translucent? Shining with colored light? Solid? Feel a sense of his energy. Ask him to reveal it to you. Is he pulsing? Emanating? Filled with energy channels or currents? Moving up and down? Back to front? Right to left? In and out? Allow him to transmit his energy signature fully to you; let it expand and encompass you as deeply as it feels comfortable. In other words, get a sense of how the archetype feels. Note the power behind the emanation so that, when this energy wishes to contact you, or vice versa, you will recognize it.

Observe how you feel in The Magician's energy. Happy? Familiar? Large? Solid? Open? Concentrated? Remember this feeling and reactivate it during spiritual practices. This emanation helps you sort things out and alter negative emotions, behaviors, and beliefs. It aligns you with your greatest potential. Known as the Higher Self, it is a great source of spiritual knowledge.

Now that you are on The Magician's frequency, breathe deeply and focus on sensing the energy in a continual way. Once you feel yourself grounded and fully in his energy field, continue by focusing on the Wand, Cup, Sword, and Pentacle; you will see your own soul's version of them. You can ask The Magician to show you what you need to know at this time about each. Note how they appear; ask him for a message.

Next, concentrate your attention on the Wand. It corresponds to your will and true aspiration. The element is fire, and the initiation is courageous consecration and dedication. Ambition evolves into aspiration. Behold your Wand. It is your branch from the Tree of Life.

The Cup, or chalice, equates with an open, loving heart. The element is water, and the initiation is purification and stabilization of the emotional life. You can focus on this Cup to attain emotional balance and center yourself in the heart of faith. It will raise your emotion to devotion. Behold your Cup. It is the beauty of your soul.

Action with integrity and truth correspond to the air element's Sword. The sword needs to be strong and sharp; therefore the qualities of justice, honorable choices, integration of polarities, and balance between mercy and severity are the strong, incorruptible materials for its making. Behold your own Sword of power.

The Pentacle, a symbol of humanity encircled by divinity, represents the secret of Spirit concealed within form and matter. The Pentacle will help you attain manifestation of your desires. Behold the Pentacle that is your golden talisman of abundance.

This meditation is very powerful. It awakens and vivifies your innate magical nature. The symbols may spontaneously appear during dreams and meditation. Since you have developed a code (symbol and meaning) for each, they will present themselves when they are invoked and when your Higher Self wishes to communicate with you about a specific subject. They all have a special, distinct spiritual feel to them. When they appear in your readings, it is a signal that the specific aspect and power is involved with the question.

The Magician ultimately represents an initiation as a spiritual adept. Now that you have discovered the tools, it is up to you to continue to cultivate your life and become the Great Work.

THE HIGH PRIESTESS

I have directed my soul toward her, and in purity have found her; having my heart fixed on her from the outset, I shall never be deserted.
(ECCLESIASTICUS 51:20)

Hidden interaction between the spiritual and personal realms is represented in this mysterious Arcanum. The High Priestess is the sovereign of the soul; she is guardian and governor of the sacred knowledge contained within it. Water flows from her skirt and, in some versions of the card, an ocean lies hidden behind her veils. The transmission of soul knowledge flows via unseen channels, currents, and telepathic waves.

The cardinal virtue of prudence is associated to The High Priestess. In the Greek and Hebrew mystery schools, prudence meant depth of intuition and an insightful gift that created prophetic (providentia) and clairvoyant, forward sight or seership. In this aspect, The High Priestess represents divine providence, grace, the Akashic Records, and the movement of the Shekinah and Holy Spirit. Hers is the essence of divine power experienced as miracles, mysteries, and rapture.

The presence of The High Priestess in your reading heralds a deepened devotion to your spirituality and the treatment of yourself and your life experiences with profound sacredness, the powers of wisdom and destiny held secret by your subconscious until the time for the soul's revelation has arrived.

Meditate on this Arcanum to deepen your relationship to your soul life of dreams, visions, psychic faculties, spiritual dimension, and gifts of the Spirit.

Interpretation

Dignity; purity of heart, mind, and action. Inner peace through alignment with personal integrity. Hold to your principles; regard them with the high esteem they deserve. Be unaffected by the projections of others. Stay quiet and serene. Treat yourself with profound sacredness. An aspect of the soul's intent and design is involved with the question.

Reversed meaning: Tainted intentions, not treating yourself as sacred; self-violation. Need to listen to subconscious messages through noting and analyzing dreams and unconscious behaviors. Lack of clarity concerning personal truth and an inability to understand soul and potentials.

Questions to Consider

- Is this involvement what my divine destiny and spiritual parents would want for me?

- What do I need to know about the hidden circumstances behind this matter?

- What is hidden deep within me, prompting me to delve into my memory?

- What mystery regarding my soul is veiled from me at this time?

- How can I best maintain my values and integrity regarding this matter? How can I be true to myself?

- Is it time for me to explore and deepen my connection to Goddess wisdom?

- Is this good or bad for my soul?

Affirmations

I remember who I truly am and where I come from.

I remember the part of me that remains in the consciousness of the divine.

I am holy.

I am virtue.

Meditation

The purpose of the High Priestess meditation is to purify your emotions and energy field in preparation for communing with your sacred self. The trump features the concept of purification and the archetype of the virgin. The way to understand these concepts is to regard them as the essence of your soul that has never left Divinity and is inviolate—untainted by life and other people. Hypnotic music, waves, and water sounds are all appropriate accompaniments for this meditation.

The Temple of Wisdom

Begin by relaxing and performing pranayama or deep relaxing breaths. Feel yourself enter into a receptive, tranquil state of peace. Continue to breathe rhythmically while asking The High Priestess to come to you. Sense the majesty of her growing close. When you have made clear contact, ask her to take you to her Temple of Wisdom. This location may be a traditional temple, a site of priestess power in the ancient world, or perhaps a cave or a hidden mountain or grove.

Enter the temple. Inside is a pool of safe, warm, inviting water. This is where you will immerse yourself for purification and cleansing of the energy field around and within you. Immerse yourself in the water in any way that you feel comfortable—bathe, wade, or swim. As you interact, affirm that you are being cleansed of all that needs purification. Feel the water cleanse you completely.

When you are ready, leave the water and proceed to a second pool that is filled with the pure water of renewal and rebirth. Immerse yourself, allowing the pool of purity and baptism into your energy field. Note your response to these sacred waters.

You can return to these pools whenever you need to be cleansed of unwanted emotional conditions and the unwanted energies of other people, places, and things. This practice is especially important for those who work with other people's psyches and health—psychics and healers. The meditation provides a balanced, cleansed, and open energy field for spiritual work.

THE EMPRESS

She gives kindly gifts to men
Smiles are always on her lovely face,
And lovely is the bright glow
That plays over the countenance.
(HOMERIC HYMN X)

A crowned woman of substance and grace is seated comfortably amid the garden of life. She is the embodiment of the fertility and imagination that has produced the field of plentitude. Her pregnancy indicates the successful and powerful blending of masculine and feminine; she is the creative principle managed with beneficence, awareness of natural timing, and competence.

The second degree of Masonic initiation, known as Fellowcraft, is symbolized by "an ear of corn near to a fall of water." Sheaves of grain, sacred to Demeter, grow in the foreground of this trump. A waterfall symbolic of the outpouring of spiritual nourishment upon the "ripening" of your aspirations as they continue to grow and multiply appears in the background of the card.

Interpretation

The power of love. Unconditional love is very powerful and healing. Love and nurture yourself, and strive to cultivate harmony in managing your personal and professional life. Open your heart. Love-filled self-acceptance attracts the birth of new conditions as you visualize yourself in a state of empowerment in the here and now. Honor yourself through the power of your own self-esteem.

Self-esteem, deservedness, openheartedness. Express your self-love confidently; flow with creative ideas. Achieving success through affectionate, pleasant, gracious, supportive, strong yet loving means. Positive, nurturing conditions prevail. Living well, thriving. Increased abundance.

The "ripening." Successful gestation of enterprises. Enrichment through experiencing life's sensual pleasures. Enjoyment of life. Development and refinement of social skills and graces. Celebrations. Happy, loving, sharing relationships. Marriage, happy alliances.

Artistic productions of all types. Capacity to create beauty. Cultural power through the arts; enhanced life values. Societal causes that nurture the best traits in humankind. Harmonization and peacemaking. Positive maternity.

Love and abundance. Harmonious and spiritual subconscious and conscious patterns of constructive, creative, imaginative, and loving ways bestow bountiful conditions.

Reversed meaning: A hope, dream, or desire is failing because it is in a hostile, unconducive, unsustaining environment. Unhappiness, destructive behavior, infertile conditions. An inability to love yourself.

Questions to Consider

- What aspect of my life needs nurturance?

- How do I access this nurturance?

- What is my body trying to tell me through its feelings, desires, discomforts, habits, and seeking of pleasures?

- What area of my life is functioning well? Where in myself am I confident, capable, and adept? What does this tell me about how I can apply this experience and its lessons to the less successful areas of my life?

- What am I creating with my thoughts? My beliefs? To what am I giving my life force?

- I conceive what I believe. How does this statement reflect my situation?

- Am I open to the flow and abundance of love and prosperity? Do I understand that I create my life moment by moment?

- How am I developing and nurturing what I've created—i.e., tending my garden?

- How do I feel about my creativity?

- How do I regard the giving and receiving of love in my life?

Affirmations

I open my heart and life to the flow of abundance and love.

I affirm that I possess the divine connection to imagine my desires into being.

I am at peace with my life and my past. I accept and love myself as I am today.

The divine life power pours its energy and light into the manifestation of my goal.

I love myself; I approve of myself; I deserve.

Meditation

The purpose of The Empress meditation is to learn and utilize effective visualization techniques. The secret to successful visualization is to focus on the attribute of divine intention behind the desire. When effectively imagined, it will simply, through the law of attraction, bring the appropriate container of your desires to you.

Most creative visualization techniques instruct you to picture yourself in the here and now in the desired state. This practice does have merit. However, if you have unconscious programming that believes you don't deserve what you are visualizing, then it cannot conceive of the desire. You will not manifest your intent, no matter how much or how effectively you can picture it. This is why a healthy conception or pregnancy is symbolized by The Empress. She has achieved successful conception of the creative imaginative seed. It has taken root and will produce desirable results.

It is more effective to focus first on the divine will and intention that would naturally produce your desired result. Self-acceptance, self-worth, and love—qualities that will, once successfully conceived, birth the desired results—are the character traits that come from the realization of the love Divinity has for you.

The Empress meditation has two parts. The first locates and dissolves disempowering beliefs (much as a gardener weeds the flower patch), and the second entails planting loving positive thoughts using visualization and affirmation. Choose a Major Arcanum that personifies the fulfillment you seek for the second part of the practice.

Releasing Negative Beliefs

The first step in the meditation is to define a life area where you are feeling deprivation—love, money, creativity, etc. This practice allows your unconscious to present you with programming to dissolve negative beliefs as you react, create, and respond to your visualization. You'll need a pen, a small piece of paper, and matches. Perform this part of the meditation outdoors in your favorite natural setting during the daytime. If you can't get outdoors, visualize a pleasant landscape.

The scene is filled with nature's activity—sunshine, birds singing, and the scents of flowers and ripening grain. Experience this location with all your senses. Seat yourself and relax into the welcoming setting. Make sure you are feeling comfortable.

Now take a few minutes to observe the flow of life surrounding you—growing, blooming, shining, etc. Simply be in its natural essence and expression. Notice the contrast with all that surrounds you—nature's harmony and abundance, and your perceived "lack."

Focus on the topic of your deprivation. Write the subject down on a piece of paper and burn it. Ask that the belief that supports it be released. Affirm the healing of your original misconception by stating: "I affirm and receive the power of divine light and love to dissolve this old, outworn, mistaken condition." Visualize white light around your false pattern, dissolving the old negativity, and ask for total release while you watch it burn.

Envision yourself surrounded by loving, healing light. Call upon this same cosmic light and love to form a new image, feeling, knowing, and thinking in your consciousness to support the true law of abundance that is your spiritual birthright. Use an appropriate Major Arcana card—The Empress herself, The Emperor, etc.—for this part of the practice. Experience yourself expectant and feeling receptive and fulfilled by the power of divine love. Picture this as a vision, and see or sense radiating light rays, energy vortices, pillars, or other shapes forming and emanating love to you.

Now you are in a state of readiness for the second part of the meditation.

Nurturing Positive Thoughts

Now place the card that you've chosen to represent your fulfillment in front of you. Each of the Major Arcana is designed to activate, integrate, and initiate you into a divine potential. The affirmations for each Major Arcanum will help you focus your request. The same rule applies as for all readings. Whether you are planning a pregnancy, a partnership, or a commitment, carefully choose the appropriate qualities in harmony with your desires.

Visualize the archetype; see white, golden, or other-colored light pulsing within the image. See that light emanate to you, and embrace and penetrate you. Breathe life into it; become it. Ask for your Higher Power's love, light, and life to enter you, then picture the whole image life-sized, or even larger than life. Remain in this state of wholeness for five to ten minutes, then affirm: "Not my will, but thy will be done, this or better, Spirit." Now offer your request up to the Divine. Always surround your visualization with light and affirm you are open to the manifestation of the Higher Power's plan.

Your idea of how your request will manifest may not align with what your destiny has in store for you. Have faith and patience. Remember, The Empress's pregnancy also symbolizes waiting for nature to take its course. All will come to fruition and be born in its destined natural time.

The secret of successful visualization and affirmation is revealed in The Empress meditation. The reason we use the archetypes of the twenty-two Major Arcana for the practice is that they are representations of all the universal potencies available to us. Your visualizations using them will activate profound experiences, since they are real powers and agents for change. The gifts of the universe will flow into your life by using this twofold process of releasing the past and inviting empowering love and abundance to take on new life through the Tarot archetypes, divine light, and meditation.

THE EMPEROR

Good Hopes, we best accomplish may, by laboring in a constant way.
(GEORGE WITHER)

The Emperor is the archetypal image of the "Christ" principle. The word Christ means "true light." He is the indwelling spiritual ego, the Master causing right instruction and goodwill to be done within the temple.

The Emperor is the master builder who designed his temple using a blueprint based on soul destiny and a moral compass. He arrived at this honored station of life through successful self-government derived from authoring his authentic destiny, based on alignment with the divine intention instilled within his heart. Self-governing and author of his own personal constitution, he answers to a higher authority.

The Master Mason, as an example of spiritual mastery, is keenly aware of assisting humanity. He possesses benevolence, kindness, and tenderness, and can also be firm and severe. He lives in the world and has mastered his lower nature and emotions. His empowerment includes the control of his mind to keep it on a positive wavelength, and to enable him to reach into the inner planes for guidance.

Interpretation

The Emperor symbolizes empowerment and the firm establishment of our birthright of independence and expression of an authentic life. Proficiency concerning the possession and use of power.

The masterful character qualities of proportion, strength, structural integrity, harmony, function, and gauging—i.e., assessment and specificity—are attributed to his worldly station of established empowerment. Autonomy, leadership, authenticity, and independence. Self-government.

Externalization and embodiment of inner potential. Power of manifestation; the plan or idea reaches form. Tangible measurable results from positive, correct intent. Capacity to rule over what has been created. Stability and permanence. The solid form, firmness, stabilization, and maturation. Sight, insight, reason; "seeing equals being." Practical, well-measured judgment or faculties.

The patriarch who governs well during peace and strife. Father figure; a mature, competent leader. The head of a project, organization, family, household; the ruling force, the authority figure.

Reversed meaning: Inability to manifest true potential in a constant, constructive way. Imitation; without authenticity. Building a life based on a faulty foundation. Goals based on beliefs from outside the authentic self have produced ego frailty, weakness, lack of self-knowledge, and little or no relationship with spiritual and soulful values. Controlling rather than personal empowerment, which includes addressing the feeling, human side of life. Father complex; difficulty handling the external, empowered world of responsibility and authority.

Questions to Consider

- What facts and beliefs constitute my personal credo?

- What principles comprise my worldview? Are they clear, true, accurate, and fair, or biased, negative, or subjectively based on other people's opinions?

- How have I governed my resources, energy, drive, and ambitions?

- How do I regard male authority figures? How do these feelings reflect on the way I honor my own authority and policies as I manage my life?

Affirmations

I see the presence of God in all I view. I act based on the will of God in all I do.

I see through God's eyes to know the divine intent behind and within every manifested matter.

My reasoning is supported by my intuition.

I am the author of my creations.

I am the authority to which I answer.

I build my temple from the principles of love, truth, and God's will for me.

I base my creations upon the celestial template of who I really am.

Meditation

The purpose of this meditation is alignment with your true self. This is the inner light that contains your destiny, also known as the blueprint of Providence. Once the centering upon your authenticity is firmly established, your life, actions, and aspirations will be constructed in alignment with your personal truth. This also brings clarity, insight, and increased intuitive awareness that will accompany and enhance your reasoning faculty.

Because The Emperor corresponds with the zodiac sign of Aries, which represents the dawn or birth, it is powerful to perform the meditation at sunrise or while watching a sunrise.

Aligning Your True Self

Begin with the usual breathing and relaxation techniques. After you feel calm and centered, focus on the Sun for a moment, then close your eyes and imagine its golden light filling and washing your eyes with light. Allow ample time for the washing to occur. Then see the Sun blazing in your navel or solar plexus area. Hold the energy there and breathe into it. This will clarify your power and align you with your true nature.

Finish the meditation by experiencing the sunlight beaming out of your eyes and navel, filling the energy around your body with golden light.

This practice will clear falseness from your intuition and reasoning faculties, and connect the power source of the true inner light to accurate perception so you can see clearly and walk your destined path.

THE HIEROPHANT

O truly sacred Mysteries! O pure Light! I am led by the light of the torch to the view of heaven and of God. I become holy by initiation. The Lord Himself is the hierophant who, leading the candidate for initiation to the Light, seals him and presents him to the Father to be preserved forever.

(CLEMENT OF ALEXANDRIA)

A Tarot costume party was held at the first World Tarot Congress. At it, one of the participants appeared dressed in full Hierophant regalia. "There's only one Hierophant!" he proclaimed as he presented himself to the costume-party judges. His friend was dressed as the skeleton from the Death card (the Hierophant reappears in many versions of that Arcanum).

Afterward, the man told me he had chosen to attend as this particular Tarot character because he hated The Hierophant! This is not an uncommon reaction to the card. To many people, it represents restrictive, religious dogma, confusion about ritual and regalia, hypocrisy, and a severe and judgmental experience with orthodox hierarchies.

The man was encouraged by his friend (Mr. Death) to attend a lecture I was presenting about initiation and The Hierophant.

He wanted him to learn that this trump also represents the metaphysical, secret, spiritual teachings available to those who aspire to look beyond the exterior of traditional doctrines. He discovered the card's esoteric meaning of the development of a real, valued relationship with a spiritual source and how his personal pathway functions.

Interpretation

Institutions and hierarchies are of benefit to you. Play by the rules and be aware of the principle and values involved with the situation; they will assist you.

A desire for spiritual "knowing." Practice of a personal, daily philosophy is encouraged. Align with the spiritual teachings, eternal truths, and principles that are of value to you.

Intuitive guidance from your Inner Guide is trustworthy. Religious beliefs and spiritual regimens will benefit you. Consult with trusted guides, teachers, healers, and counselors. Teaching, coaching, and consultant professions are indicated.

Reversed meaning: Unconventional, explorative, inventive, and unusual experiences. Explore original and unique opportunities if surrounded by positive cards. This card can also signal not heeding intuitive promptings or synchronistic messages. Hubris, superficiality, and materialism if surrounded by negative cards, as well as an inability to perceive spiritual sources and resources.

Questions to Consider

- What motivates me to connect with my spiritual source?

- How can I practice the disciplines that will keep me aligned with my spiritual quest?

- How do I make room in my life and myself for the wisdom within me to emerge?

Affirmations

I build and sustain my spiritual life, my temple, on the foundation of eternal spiritual truths.

I grow wise through my spiritual devotions.

My inner self now connects to the guidances from my Higher Self.

I listen to the still small voice and become one with its source.

Meditation

Mystical teachings are available to anyone who seeks knowledge. Having a clear definition of your specific link with Divinity is like being handed a road map to a well-worn path trod by many initiates before you. The Hierophant meditation will reveal your spiritual path, and its practices, traits, lessons, and blessings. There are three distinct pathways tread by the initiate. The meditation's purpose is to help you discover your soul path or style of spirituality. Each path has particular gifts and ways to know inner wisdom teachings. Refer to the journal worksheet at the end of this section to record your experience after you perform this meditation.

The Entrance to the Temple

Plan to spend some time with this meditation. Play a piece of music that you feel has a particularly holy atmosphere, or reminds you of a temple or holy place in nature. You may choose to have someone guide you through the visualization by reading it to you and asking the questions. You may also choose to record the meditation first, then play it back during your session.

Relax and center yourself with the pranayama, or rhythmic, breathing. Ask your master teacher, Inner Guide, guardian angel, or Higher Self to be present. Visualize and sense that you are in a sacred place in nature or in a temple. When comfortably ensconced, ask your guide to take you to the Hall of Initiation so you can seek wisdom and truth about your soul path.

See a portal or doorway. "Know Thyself" is written on the lintel above the entrance. Enter into the temple's antechamber. This is a small room adjacent to the main hall. A white robe is waiting for you. Place the garment around you; note how it feels.

You are aware that a great hall or sacred setting lies beyond this small room, but, for now, you are to stay in the antechamber. Feel your guide's presence growing stronger and remember to breathe rhythmically. A desk with an open book, a pen, and a lit candle stands before you. A chair awaits you. Be seated, all the while feeling the loving presence of your guide. Answer the following questions. Write them in the book of your life before you:

- Are you sincerely ready and desirous of entering the Initiation Hall?

- Why do you seek admittance?

Write the answers, then sign and date the entry. If you are ready, you will feel your guide's presence grow stronger.

It is now time to enter the main temple room. This is the first Hall of Initiation. When you are ready, you are welcome to enter. Before you, you will see three closed doors. View each one individually. The first has a pulsing life force emanating from it and bears the emblem of a heart. The second seems to be breathing and has two crossed keys upon it. The third emanates a great light and has an eye on its surface.

Now request to know which path you are on. Ask your guide and feel yourself drawn to one of the three doors. When you are ready, go to the door, open it, and enter. Observe what you are shown. This information can come in the form of a sensation, feeling, thought, vision, or sound. Experience what is inside the chamber. Are there angels? A presence? Symbols? Colors? Lights? Or perhaps Tarot archetypes that have been working on your path with you? Ask for deeper understanding regarding who they are and what messages they bring. Request deeper insight about this path. Ask about its current teaching and the lessons that your everyday life experience has brought to you. You can pose a question regarding a situation and receive guidance. What about this path do you need to understand? What do you need to do to steady yourself and proceed further?

Thank the guides and teachers for their presence. Bring the emblem (heart, eye, or key) into your heart, third eye, or crown. See where it wants to be placed—at your heart, third eye, etc. Return to the antechamber. Remove the white robe and, as you do, feel your usual identity grow strong. Then breathe normally and sense your surroundings. Leave the chamber and temple, knowing your Higher Self, guides, and teachers are there for you to call upon for further exploration of the temple.

Feel yourself returning to normal consciousness. Record your impressions or write them on the journal worksheet at the end of this section. Review the meditation as a reference point for your experience. Study the Interpretation section for further explanation of your meditation.

Personal Soul Path

The three paths of this meditation must all be walked and integrated. The three ways of knowing they represent exist within us all. When the three paths are trod over time on the journey to know your spiritual nature, you attain a new level called Direct Cognition and receive the knowledge and conversation with The Hierophant—the Holy Guardian Angel, Higher Self, Master, and Teacher. When you reach a state of complete "knowing," you become The Hierophant.

The inner teacher, or esoteric facet of The Hierophant, is an aspect of your own soul that is interested in your spiritual progression. It dwells within the center of your being. It acts as a mentor, saint, or sage, and stays in contact with you, subconsciously or consciously guiding you on your path.

The Path of the Rose

The path symbolized by the heart is known as the Path of the Rose. It is a devotional way to experience Divinity—prayerful and filled with openheartedness. It especially represents feeling compassion, healing gifts, and giving service to others in the form of heartfelt caring, nurturing, teaching, and loving. "Tho I have all knowledge and have not love, I am nothing." Love seeks to see and envision God in all humanity, regardless of externals. As your heart and mind fix themselves continually upon holding the idea of good, the nature of your self and your broadened relationship with Divinity knows love in a personal and transpersonal way. This approach, mainly through "the adoration of the heart," develops the Pillar of Strength, love's ultimate value.

The tests of this pathway are the emotional addictions that distract you from devotion. The challenge is to refuse to be run by them and to offer them up to the Higher Powers to dissolve and release. The power of spiritual love and self-love is the solution to the challenge of this path.

Consider the use of body disciplines for steadying your emotions. This may be exercise, yoga, Tai Chi, or breathing techniques. Meditation walks also help, as do prayers, affirmations, and visualizations. Doing for others, the environment, or animals, and caring acts of kindness also heal the lower aspect of this path. Studying and consciousness-raising can also help balance an overly emotional state.

The Path of the Crossed Keys

The crossed keys represent the Path of Spirit in Action and The Actor. Spirituality is physical and experiential. Awareness is sensed and experience is felt. Your physical body becomes a vehicle to know the divine. The individuals on this path are the "doers," the makers and builders.

Spiritual movement—dance, gardening, nature trips, healthy lifestyles, ecology, earth mysteries, sacred architecture, artistic endeavors, and sacred spaces—are ways to trod this path. Enactment of rituals corresponds to the path of action. People worshipping the Sun god at Stonehenge at a solstice express the spirituality experienced through the body in sacred time and space at an Earth ceremony.

The practice of yoga, Tai Chi, and other spiritually based exercises and postures, as well as mental techniques of communication with the body, the chakras, and energy currents create a body-mind link and endow the participant with intuitive powers.

A spiritual tradition in which actors participate in rituals, plays, and dioramas—including the portrayal of Tarot characters and scenes—is another way to experience self-awareness. In the mystery schools, roles are assigned and participants have to "get into character." The idea is that you become the role so that, subsequently, you realize that capacity in yourself. This brings you an awareness of untapped inner potential and newfound abilities and resources.

For example, undertaking the role of The Empress develops kindness. The Emperor brings out mastery and authority. Simply choose the Arcanum, then create the environment and costume. And, most important, get into the character. Feel, think, and believe you are it. The physical enactment of the character serves as both evocation and invocation. The power within is expressed, and the gods reach out to meet it. You discover your human powers, and as you integrate them into your life, magic happens.

The challenging side of the Path of Spirit in Action is the inability to find the meaning behind the practice, doing without thinking, or lack of introspection. This causes you to perceive your physical body and the material world as the only reality and to have a life without true purpose or to lead an unquestioned life.

The Path of the Lily

The eye symbolizes the Path of the Lily. This is the path of contemplation, where meditation, listening, receptivity, awakenings, silences, and openness produce personal realization. The individuals on this path have a love of the divine word. They cherish learning opportunities, especially conferences. Study, contemplation of a Tarot card, teaching, writing, speaking, and understanding is how this path of the soul operates.

The path working involves awareness of what the topic contemplated evokes within you. Then that revelation takes you to your own personal truth. The passive act of moving inward involves feeling the essence of what is being contemplated. This produces a movement away from ego into the realm of the Higher Self, where visions and ecstasy can be attained.

The challenge of this type is thinking and studying theory, but avoiding experience—too much in the head or mind, with little interest in the experiential or feeling realm. For those on the Path of the Lily, the key is to keep an open heart, so that you can feel what you contemplate. For example, it is one thing to study a philosophic principle and quite another to experience one of the teachings firsthand.

Soul Path Worksheet

Completing the worksheet on pages 151–152 will give you a great deal of information for journaling, discussion, or contemplation. We each find our own spiritual way. This meditation will help you learn yours. Refer to the guidance about your path and explore the information given above as you answer these questions. Know that you can move from one path to another, and eventually experience all three.

Date:_____

1. Are you on the Path of the Rose, the Path of Spirit in Action, or the Path of the Lily?

   _____

   _____

2. What are the qualities associated with this path? (Refer to the text.)

   _____

   _____

3. How do these principles apply to your life?

   _____

   _____

   _____

4. How does this make you feel?

   _____

   _____

   _____

5. How can you facilitate this path?

   _____

   _____

6. What did you encounter inside the Hall of Initiation?

_____

_____

7. What did you experience in the antechamber as you wrote your purpose in the book of your life?

_____

_____

_____

8. Did you feel your guide's presence? What was this experience like for you?

_____

_____

_____

9. How can you focus, consolidate, and proceed with your dedication to personal spiritual path working?

_____

_____

_____

THE LOVERS

Raphael is charged to heal the earth and through him the earth furnishes an abode for man whom he also heals of his maladies.

(THE ZOHAR)

The Lovers symbolize a mystical practice known as *kything*, an ancient Scottish word that means "to appear without disguise," "to be manifest." Kything is a method of spiritual presence whose purpose is to bring about a loving spiritual connection, union, or communion between two or more persons or beings without the spoken word.

This communion takes place in the spiritual world, in a way similar to prayer and meditation. It is a relationship in which two people know the meaning of what is being expressed. It is based on the idea of Oneness. To participate in kything, you must be sensitive, able to intuit intention, openhearted, and delighted with the ecstasy of the experience.

The Lovers trump illustrates the complete honesty of kything. According to the mystic Swedenborg, when we experience Oneness, we appear without pretense or disguising intents or thoughts. It is the only way spiritual angels can present themselves to each other.

The power of spiritual discernment—in other words, the ability to see into the spiritual realms and vice versa—is a result of kything. And it is this ability that has enabled the Archangel Raphael to be perceived by The Lovers.

Interpretation

The Lovers indicate a happy relationship or union with the beloved. A conscious connection with a larger reality of spirit, nature, and life is experienced through the mystery of falling in love. The erotic power within your nature is stirred, and your heart leaps to the sharing of life's energies. When The Lovers appear, the attraction offers an opportunity to grow and know yourself through a "significant other." The mystery of sexual relations as a loving communion, both reproductive and mystical (tantra), is allocated to The Lovers trump.

Lessons are involved with the law of attraction. You have attracted someone into your life who provides a balance. The power and spirit of love attract supportive loving contacts that enhance and evolve your life.

The Lovers can indicate a harmonious relationship in your life. Sincerity, trust, genuine love, and a balance of intimacy and individuality are indicated. Creation and cultivation of all types of positive relationships bring the blossoming of the potential within your spirit, mind, and body. Development and expansion of relationships that reflect your true values enhance your self-esteem.

Love is understood as the "power" of the life source and healing. Learn healing techniques or receive a healing. The healing of relationships between individuals or the inner aspects of your self is successful. Accurate discernment of that which is healthy; correct choices.

Reversed meaning: The Lovers reversed indicate poor choices. This card's reversal can represent relationship interference from others, or from inner conflicts. Poor communication exacerbates the problem. The Lovers reversed represent disconnection with life and nature, and an inability to feel or acknowledge feelings resulting in a lack of intimacy, loneliness, and alienation. A breakdown of family and important relationships; an inability to communicate requires a mediator, counselor, or expert consultant.

Questions to Consider

- How do I nourish my relationship with the God of my own understanding?

- Do I choose what is correct for me with faith and guidance from my Higher Self?

- Am I choosing self-love and self-worth over someone else's needs and problems?

- How do the situations and people I attract reflect my internal relationship with my heart, mind, practicality, and spirit?

- Do my relationships reflect self-love, or fearfulness and a lack of self-worth?

Affirmations

I am loved and loving.

The Archangel Raphael heals my body, mind, and spirit.

The Archangel Raphael heals my relationship with my Beloved.

I am known by my spiritual heart.

I choose that which is balanced and healthy.

I am open to the intimate relationship between me and my loved one.

Meditation

The purpose of The Lovers meditation is the healing of relationships. A happy partnership is symbolized in the trump. A longing for the spiritual love union with your soul mate colors your life and is a primary motivation for your relationships. You know or sense that devoted unconditional love, communion with spiritual powers, and supportive and creative relationships exist, or you wouldn't feel such longing for and recognition of them when they come to you or you witness and respond to them.

In the first part of this meditation, the Archangel Raphael, the great healing emissary of God, is summoned to heal both internal and external relationships by the removal of disempowering beliefs that separate you from the tangible fulfillment of your heart's desire. The second part invites Archangel Raphael to bless you and your relationship.

Healing Disempowering Beliefs

Perform the usual breathing and relaxation. Imagine yourself in a garden or natural setting during the daytime, resplendent with sunshine. (This meditation can also be performed outdoors in a park, garden, woodland, or forest.) Visualize or feel the Sun's warming rays and the Earth firmly under your feet.

Focus your breath and attention at your solar plexus or navel area. This chakra deals with emotional and power issues and is usually where the split from wholeness that separates you from your desired happiness is stored. This center's element is fire. It is masculine and has a yellow color vibration. Continue to focus on your solar plexus or navel center. Breathe into it and, as you do, allow the yellow of the Sun to become golden. Then experience the Sun growing larger. Feel the heat and light radiating in your belly.

Focus on your crown center area. Feel it warm and aglow with more golden light. Spend a few minutes breathing into your crown chakra; then, when you are ready, concentrate on the space directly above your head.

See an orb of white light above your head, then ask that the presence of the Archangel Raphael come into the light. As the Archangel's essence enters the space, you'll feel an energetic shift or see, hear, or otherwise experience his presence.

Next, bring the energy into your prepared crown chakra, then into your solar plexus via your heart. Allow your entire being to become a column of gold-and-white healing light.

Ask and affirm that the disempowering separation, split, or wound between you and your natural birthright of fulfillment and connection to your spiritual power be melted or burned away through the regenerating, transforming aspects of fire and Sun. Ask

the Archangel Raphael to heal you permanently of all disempowering beliefs, feelings, and habits. You do not have to name or even
know the beliefs; Raphael, with his power of kything, will know
where they lie.

New Empowerment

In the next part of the meditation, you will request to experience
the empowerment of balanced love within you, toward others, and
ultimately in union with the Divine. Feel the kything quality of
unspoken, heartfelt knowing between you and Raphael, between
the male and female. Now return the feeling from your heart, for
this is the true miracle of love that heals.

You now have this energy signature in your magnetic field.
Therefore, you will attract the same toward you. Your heart is now
your ally for discernment of that which is true and for your highest
good, especially regarding choices and with relationships.

Ask for a final blessing and healing from Archangel Raphael.
Know that, as you do this, your alignment prepares you for opening the chambers of your heart to spiritual powers, creativity, and
conscious union with the Divine. Thank Raphael for the blessing
and then see the white orb disappear. Feel your crown and solar
plexus areas close. Return to normal breathing and become aware
of your surroundings. Revisit and repeat this meditation when you
want to make important decisions or choices, or require correct
discernment.

THE CHARIOT

*The Self is the Rider in the chariot of the body, of which the senses
are horses and the mind the reins.*
(BHAGAVAD-GITA)

The Chariot represents your soul's triumphant emergence as driver or charioteer of your life. The Emperor and Charioteer share the symbolism of armor and have triumphed in the battles of life. The Emperor represents the inner light of your soul's blueprint of destiny. The Charioteer is that destiny's driver; he knows the road map and has successfully navigated your authentic self to a level of full expression.

A new journey is being prepared—a deeper foray into the quest for further soul development—and the sojourner requires a technique for protection. The soul has a sensitive and wide vibration field, and it requires safeguarding so it can open to fulfill its purpose. Protection techniques aid you as you penetrate the new realms of universal vibration and Providence continues to grace you.

Interpretation

The Chariot represents arrival at a goal, successful conclusion, and accomplishment. A heroic victory over internal or external foes and obstacles has occurred through strength of character, perseverance, and faith.

The appearance of The Chariot in a reading suggests the attainment of self-mastery and the restoration of serenity, creativity, initiative, and a faithful heart. A new cycle of self-honoring and recognition for achievements commences. Heroic reclamation of the authentic self produces peace and newfound security.

Lessons have been learned, especially concerning emotional imbalance and limitations of beliefs and thoughts. The past has been conquered. A catharsis has occurred, and the suffering that results from addictive emotions and behaviors ceases.

Communicate or speak from your own experience to enlighten other people. The opportunity to assume responsibility and power in your own field of expertise will be beneficial. Destined and favorable forces benefit you.

Reversed meaning: An attempt to force and egotistically control conditions and people; riding roughshod over anything that stands in the way. There may be emotional problems caused by weak boundaries, defensive behavior, and unconscious conditioning. An energy field that is too open and weak leads to violation and invasiveness from other people's energy. Stored negative, blocked anger and frustration can cause turmoil in emotional and physical health and prevent true empowerment.

Questions to Consider

- What are my past accomplishments?

- How can I apply my positive character traits used in the past to help me accomplish my current goal?

- How does the overcoming of negativity make me feel?

- How do I feel when I speak out from my own experience and expertise, when I know I have something of value and meaning to say?

- What do I do to ensure protection for my mind, my feelings, and my body?

- What happens when I overprotect myself and live in the past?

Affirmations

I am perfectly protected.

My soul takes ascendance in my life.

I allow myself to release all emotional beliefs and behaviors that no longer serve my evolved self.

Meditation

When the soul becomes the prime mover in your life, the gifts of the Spirit emerge—psychic talents, spiritual powers, and their purpose. With them comes a test—a challenge not to be unbalanced by negative energies such as low-level spirits, personal fears, and invasive people that can take advantage of your power.

The first Chariot meditation will give you an easy technique for protecting and maintaining your boundaries while remaining open to spiritual resources. The second practice features the removal of unwanted energies.

Protection and Balancing

Complete your breathing and relaxation as usual. Imagine a gold light above you, then below you, then in front of you, then behind you, then to your left and right. Sense the light radiating toward you from the six directions.

Now visualize gold light emanating toward you from all the spaces between all the directions, so that you are encased within a complete egg or square of gold light. This is your protection and balancing technique. Each time you perform this simple practice, you will experience the gold light differently, and it will keep you protected from unwanted external influences. It will also keep you open to spiritual help and awareness from your Higher Self.

Banishing Unwanted Energy

Use a favorite incense, smudge stick, or herb bundle for this procedure. Decide which area you want to cleanse and prepare yourself by deep breathing and focusing on your intention. Light the incense, smudge stick, or herb bundle and, carrying it in your hand, walk around the room three times counterclockwise. Watch as the sacred smoke banishes the unwanted energy. Affirm that all negativity is expelled from the room. This simple practice will help to clear negative energy from your space.

To create a circle of protection in a room, repeat the banishment method, then walk three times around the space clockwise carrying the incense. As you walk, call upon the Higher Powers to assist you in creating and maintaining a protected space. Allow the scent and smoke to penetrate each wall and corner, and the floor and ceiling. After the third circle, place the incense in a holder and let it burn down in the room.

Leave the room. When you reenter, the energy should feel refreshed and calm.

Repeat the practice when you sense the room requires rebalancing or when someone negative has upset the space.

· 8 ·

THE MAJOR ARCANA
8–14

This series of Major Arcana cards depicts the metaphysical accomplishment of the integration of the spiritual nature into the temporal self.

STRENGTH

This thing is the strongest of all powers, the force of all forces for it overcometh every subtle thing and doth penetrate every solid substance.
(EMERALD TABLET OF HERMES)

Strength represents personal willpower blended with a deepened awareness of the Higher Power, applied toward the training of the lower nature. Courage and strength of character, used to face fears and fulfill the desires derived from the best and highest self, are symbolized by the woman's patient care toward the strong yet ferocious lion. She is powerful because she has occult energy activated through spiritual breathing and metaphysical practices to help her with her task of tending, training, and transforming the lion of instinct.

STRENGTH.

Her image is a symbolic representation of the alignment of appropriate desires based on self-esteem and spiritual love. The alignment symbolized by the chain of roses becomes the power used to tame the lion, which is actually the Alchemical lion of transformation from the lower to the Higher Self. When your self-acceptance, self-worth, and desires, all based on spiritual love, are in alignment, your life transforms powerfully. This card in a reading signals that the desires involved in the question are spiritually-based and healthy for the client.

The Strength card's appearance highlights an area of your life in which believing and acting in accordance with your highest good creates empowerment. It indicates an increased capacity to discipline and control the will through understanding and firm yet gentle behavioral adjustments. There is a quickening of power that leads to a new cycle of a higher spiritual nature. The strength meditation reveals the way to open to this spiritual power source. The body discipline of Hatha Yoga and specific breathing practices of pranayama are the essence and source of spiritual strength.

Interpretation

The Strength card indicates the forging of personal strength and practiced self-love, self-worth, and the power of courageously speaking your truth.

The seeker is developing an awareness of the relationship between himself and his Higher Self. Love, as a strengthening power, has brought him to a point where spiritual truth motivates his thoughts, words, and actions. He or she now knows that he deserves love, peace, and plenty and that he is lovable just the way he is. Desires are expressed appropriately. When this card appears, it signals a healthy, constructive desire such as satisfaction in livelihood, relationships, self-expression, prosperity, healthy living, and spiritual pursuits.

This Arcanum's appearance heralds "goodness." Advise the seeker that whatever is good for him to experience, whether this may be through adversity, character strengthening, or gentle, supportive means, may be presented to him.

Reversed meaning: There is high drama in the seeker's life. He or she may be blaming and projecting emotional issues onto other people or situations. The ego struggles, and will and desires go unfulfilled. Self-loathing creates angry, destructive behavior.

Questions to Consider

- What constitutes goodness, kindness, and understanding in my situation?
- How can I bring kindness and loving tolerance to my situation?
- How can I offer the same qualities to myself?
- Am I practicing pranic breathing to refine my energy?
- Am I being loyal to my personal oaths?

Affirmations

I love myself.

I respect myself.

I trust myself.

I am honest with myself.

I am gentle and compassionate with myself.

I appreciate myself.

I honor myself.

I enjoy myself.

I am patient with myself and celebrate my progress.

I love and accept myself as I am.

Meditation

Pranayama is the science of breathing that cultivates high frequency energy and enlivens the flow of healing energy. Refinements of the royal and noble leonine instincts are the results of pranayama.

Attention to diet, keeping the mind on spiritual matters, and the evolution of emotions to become devotions are all character-istics of an unfolding spiritualizing of the personality. Becoming noble in mind, action, and heart is essential so that the energy cul-tivated though breathing practices will be channeled into refined instincts, drives, and aspirations.

Hatha Yoga is physical exercise that will naturally and gently awaken the Kundalini or spiritual energy. Yoga means "union," the pathway to enlightenment. It is the power and secret involved with The Hierophant. It is regarded as a pristine, pure energy existent in the body in a dormant state of potentiality. At the same time, it is a spiritual power that is the source behind all matter.

As you evolve and grow strong with yoga and pranayama, you will become aware of your consciousness and how it may be stuck on issues of power, survival, or sex. The energy will rise to that level, creating dramatic, upsetting conditions. This is the real "lion tam-ing" taking place in Strength. The woman of Strength is depicted in pure white clothing to direct us to purify our lower nature by choosing a desire in harmony with the divine plan. For example, do not desire harm to yourself or another. Instead, desire peace, prosperity, and fulfillment.

It often helps to switch gears if you are working toward control of fears, anger, or self-defeating behaviors and emotions. If you have been using a mental or analytical approach to solving your problems and the condition is still unruly, switch to prayerfulness or meditation, and seek help by opening your heart and healing hurt emotions. If, on the other hand, emotional passions are what are causing you suffering, use the mind to analyze and seek the wisdom of self-healing actions.

The rule of thumb is to go up one level from where the struggle is taking place. If it is at the body level, seek help through emotions and feelings. If the struggle is at an emotional level, seek resolution through the mind and thoughts. If there is an issue of being too much in your head, seek guidance at a spiritual level. If spiritual difficulties exist, use all three aspects. It is important to be grounded when seeking help from a higher realm. To do this, visualize a cord extending from the base of your spine and firmly anchored to the earth and see and feel yourself strongly attached to the earth.

Strength takes on a new meaning as you prepare and strengthen your body, mind, and spirit through breathing and yoga. Purification of the mind and intention, selfless service, and openheartedness are the character qualities needed in order to "rise" to the good of all and the harm of none. The spiritual attitude is one of seeing the divine within all beings and serving that essence. The transformed heart and purified subconscious are prerequisites for safe opening of this power source.

Breath of Fire

This technique of breathing is a way of creating energy and settling your mind. There are both physical and mental benefits to this practice. Physically, the Breath of Fire allows the body to increase its oxygen supply while getting rid of the toxic by-products of metabolism. Mentally, this breathing technique improves focus and concentration and helps to maintain balance between the emotions and reason.

Sit in a cross-legged position with one hand on your abdomen and another on your rib cage. Inhale slowly, feeling the abdomen expand first and then the rib cage, as the breath moves into your chest. As you exhale, feel the air leaving your lower chest, then middle, then upper chest. Do a few of these slow, deep breaths to prepare you mind and body for the Breath of Fire.

Inhale through your nostrils and concentrate on moving your diaphragm down into the abdomen, drawing air into the lower part of your lungs. As you do this, keep your focus on your third chakra, at the solar plexus.

Quickly exhale, forcing the air out of your nostrils by compressing your abdominal muscles. You should hear the rapid expulsion of air through your nostrils.

Do not pause between exhaling and inhaling. Keep the rhythm of the breath going, as quickly as you can. Try to do a complete cycle of breath each second.

Keep this breathing going for one to three minutes. You may feel slight lightheadedness and some tingling sensations in fingers or toes when you do this meditation. This is completely normal and indicates that the body is adjusting to the flow of oxygen and stimulation of the nerves. If you do start to feel dizzy, then stop, and focus on the technique at a slower pace until your breathing is even and rhythmic. There should be no strain or tension while doing the Breath of Fire.

If you do this exercise regularly, you will find that you deal better with stress, have more stamina, and generally feel more balanced and relaxed.

THE HERMIT

Happy is the man that findeth wisdom and the man that getteth understanding.
For the merchant of it is better than silver and the gain thereof than fine gold.
(SOLOMON THE WISE)

Hermits were not uncommon during the Middle Ages. As humble renunciates, they lived in nature, isolated from the rigors and regalia of the traditional society and religious values. Desirous only of an intimate, direct contact with their Divinity, they dedicated heart, mind, and body to God.

The Hermit is the archetype of the Wise Man personified as a saint, as Hermes Trismegistus, as ascended Master, as the Monk, as Solomon the Wise, and as Merlin. He is Moses atop Mount Sinai receiving divine wisdom and striving to bring God's words to humanity's ears. In the Roman pantheon, he is Mercury and correlates with The Magician of the Tarot. He represents the pinnacle of The Magician's goal of attaining the Great Work.

He is Hermes, the overlord of the Hermetic arts of healing, herbalism, magic, secret knowledge, and writing. Hermes was known as the guide or shepherd of souls. As leader and protector, he is both savior and psychopomp. A psychopomp is a conductor into the spiritual realms of the soul. The Hermit trump represents this guide.

One of the most important aspects of The Hermit is your relationship with the guidance and spiritual awareness derived from your Higher Self or Inner Guide. Think of this energy as a wise overseer and companion who knows your soul and desires its progression. As the detachment from ego and its distractions occurs, you'll become aware of this subtle guide through meditation, increased intuition, and deep inner wisdom that becomes available to you.

Interpretation

Full and successful unfoldment of the potential of a person or situation. Achievement, attainment; a pinnacle is reached; a change in status and title. Independence. Hard work pays off. Humility in success. Seniority. Self-reliance.

Ascendance as an accomplished adept.

The full development of the potential of a person or situation. Competence; admirable achievements created through focus; steadfastness, discipline, and clear priorities. Expertise. A gifted visionary offers counsel and wise guidance. A blessing in the form of precise, excellent advice. Helpfulness from teachers, healers, experienced consultants, and other sincere and knowledgeable sources. Be humble and open to wisdom deeper than your own understanding.

Neutrality and wisdom; especially helpful for those who work with or encounter other people's problems. Well-developed skills of listening, analysis, synthesis, and observation. Believe in yourself; you know what is best for you. The maturity and introspection to recognize your true needs and values is available to you. Be open to receive guidance from others more learned than you. Well-integrated lessons.

Dedicated and heartfelt service to others; a purposeful sharing of wisdom to light the path for others to find their way. A "peak" experience of a heightened, mystical nature. To touch and be touched by the Divine. Power of light, intimate experience with the light body. Simplify your life in order to achieve your highest potential. A retreat and disassociation from worldly objectives brings rejuvenation and renewed connection to essential values.

Reversed meaning: Unwise actions, inexperience, not learning from prior experience or heeding advice from others who are more knowledgeable. Take time to detach from unproductive behavior and acquiring new habits that serve your Higher Self.

Questions to Consider

- Do I need to streamline my life?

- Do I need to organize and prioritize with my most sincere desire as my motivation and goal?

- Do I need to spend time alone to contemplate, learn, and tend to my spiritual well-being and articulate my personal mission?

- How do I spend my personal time?

- How do I feel when I've achieved recognition, or conquered a problem, or attained a goal?

- Do I let myself integrate a success so that I can fully assume the mantle of power?

- Am I regarding my life and my body as a temple?

- Am I comfortable being in solitude on my spiritual journey?

Affirmations

My father and I are one.

I commit my whole being to my spiritual illumination.

I am open to receive the wisdom and guidance from my spiritual guides and teachers.

I commit my whole being to my spiritual illumination. I am open to receive the wisdom and guidance from my spiritual guides and teachers.

I exist through the light of the divine presence. My entire physical being experiences the light of the divine within me. Every atom of every cell emanates the divine spark.

Meditation

The Hermit meditation connects you with your Inner Guide or Higher Self. A direct experience with this spiritual companion, Inner Guide, spirit guide, or Higher Self imparts wisdom, protection, and unconditional love from the Higher Power in an experiential way.

Tranquility and deep relaxation are prerequisites for this meditation exercise, as are total silence and total lack of interruption. Visualize or visit a quiet natural setting during the evening or nighttime. You may choose to bring a staff or walking stick, as well as a lit lantern or candle. If you perform this meditation outdoors, bring a blanket or coat with a hood so you will be warm.

Contacting Your Inner Guide

Begin by standing straight, with your feet firmly planted on the earth. Extend the staff and lantern in front of you and feel your responses to this activity. Hermit energy may be received through body sensations. You may feel a sense of expansiveness, of height, of connection to the universe or to all nature. Other sensations may occur, especially in your head. Perform deep breathing with your eyes half opened or closed, and feel the depth and breadth of the nighttime.

Now ask your spiritual guide to draw close; you will feel an energy shift. Feel its presence, sense where it stands relative to you—in front, in back, or at your side. When you are ready, ask it to touch, then intermingle with, your energy field. Note the feeling. You may wish to ask its name. This is how it feels to be in your Inner Guide's presence. The feeling may be familiar, since that presence has always been with you.

If you have a request for your guide, take the opportunity to ask or affirm your desire. Wait for a response, which may come as a telepathic knowing, a memory, a thought, as words, or in a vision. Note the method in which you receive the message, since this may represent the usual communication style that will occur between you and your guide. This will help you recognize when your guide communicates with you. A colored light, symbol, scent, sensation, or sound may accompany this "drawing close."

Now that you have experienced this connection, you can ask your Inner Guide to join you when meditating or reading the Tarot. It will also make its presence felt in important dreams and during your waking life. When you are in need, call on this presence for support, knowledge, guidance, and protection.

Close the meditation by breathing normally and becoming aware of your everyday surroundings. Take a short walk and review the information given to you, then record it in your journal. You and your guide now have conscious communication, and it will impress you with insight and guidance more frequently and easily. If you feel the communication is unclear, you can always request that the message be made more clear to you. One of the most important aspects of this card is that you can ask for guidance from your spirit guide.

THE WHEEL OF FORTUNE

A prisoner devoid of books, had he only a Tarot of which he knew how to make use, could in a few years acquire a universal science and converse with an unequalled doctrine and inexhaustible eloquence.
(ELIPHAS LEVI, *TRANSCENDENTAL MAGIC*)

WHEEL of FORTUNE.

The Wheel of Fortune was once portrayed as a wheel of chance. Happy and hapless victors and victims rode a wheel turned by the capricious hand of fate. The card represented good luck, misfortune, change, and the uncontrollable and unpredictable movement of destiny's ups and downs.

The esoteric version of the card features an orange eight-spoked wheel, an ancient symbol for the Sun and its rays. Orange is the occult color of the Sun and represents the "God force" of the solar mysteries. The solar mystery is a metaphysical belief in the existence of the divine self or inner light, and that spiritual illumination is our divine inheritance. We partake of this treasure and strive to progress toward it through systems of spiritual knowledge that hold this belief as a key precept.

The Wheel of Fortune contains symbols representative of various religions and philosophies that are based on the inner light. Alchemy, Tarot, Astrology, Qabalah, ancient Egyptian rites, and Buddhist, Christian, and Hebrew symbols are all depicted in the card. A wheel or circle represents wholeness and completion and is regarded as a "linking point" between the Earth and the cosmic planes. In the Chinese world, circles denote the "Older Heavens," while the square or cross depicts the "Younger Heavens." The Buddhist eight-spoked wheel relates to the idea of rebirth and reincarnation, and is another way to demonstrate the archetype of the cycle and the circle—time, infinity, and evolution—ascribed to the symbolism of the wheel.

The Wheel's complex design expresses the basic composition of a mandala, a symbolic diagram usually consisting of a circle, square, and other figures. It is used for meditation and represents the relationship between the spiritual and temporal worlds.

Interpretation

The arrival of an expansive opportunity. The attraction of benefactors. A cycle of new life growth begins as rewards come to fruition. Correct intent channeled into productivity yields positive, expansive results. Movement, dynamic progression toward destined evolution. Completion, fulfillment, integration. Life renews itself on a larger scale.

Readiness for success. Preparation for opportunity to occur, coupled with timing and fate. Good fortune, auspicious change. The door to a new journey is presented. Breakthroughs, wealth; fortune smiles; new marriages and alliances, careers, and launching of new life priorities. Travel.

Deeper understanding of your soul purpose and destiny. Earnest seeking for life's meaning; expanding your conscious grasp of knowledge. Open your mind and heart to philosophical and spiritual teachings that bring you joy and uplift your spirit. Cosmic learning beckons; systems of wisdom like the Tarot, astrology, Qabalah, philosophy, and religions are studied and benefit you.

Reversed meaning: Inability to understand the law of cause and effect; liberation through the same law if intention, knowledge, and action are applied.

Negative, repetitive, cyclical behavior or circumstances with their predictable results. Regression rather than progression due to faulty, limited beliefs and intentions. The big, important questions are not being asked or the message goes ignored. It is highly possible that you do not conceive of yourself as having a larger dimension or have chosen to ignore it in favor of a more predictable and smaller existence. Beware a lack of personal responsibility and avoidance of self-awareness. Indolence, laziness, cowardice, and helpless fatalism.

Questions to Consider

- How have I created and continued to sustain positive, open conditions for attraction of my goals?

- Do I believe I deserve the reward for which I ask?

- How do I reward myself?

- How do I feel when others reward and recognize me?

- Am I ready to strive, to evolve, and to pursue greater beneficial circumstances?

- Have I fallen into a rut and become complacent? Why?

- How do the results I have today reflect the efforts I made yesterday?

- Do I really understand the law of cause and effect?

- Do I have the wisdom to use the law of cause and effect to manifest my desires?

- How do my true intentions reflect causation and manifestation?

Affirmations

I am dedicated to activation of my truest cause of heart, mind, spirit, and body.

I am the divine spark that turns the Wheel. I remain centered within its essence.

I am the product of my beliefs. I believe I am a manifesting the light of divinity.

I am in perfect communion with the system of spiritual knowledge that is my teacher during this specific phase of my evolution.

I am surrounded by the circle of omniscient protection as I travel into the dimensions of the spiritual planes.

Meditation

The meditation for The Wheel introduces the idea of the Library of the Soul, an actual plane of knowledge where you can go to understand your soul lessons and powers. You'll also discover how to participate in cowriting your destiny through the wisdom of your Inner Guide, The Hermit.

As your relationship with the facets of your soul progresses, you come to understand that it has access to inner wisdom—schools and planes or realms of arcane knowledge. Edgar Cayce and other prophets accessed a dimension in the inner realms called "the Akashic Records," a repository of arcane and unconscious knowledge on the astral plane. Past soul lessons and purpose, reincarnation, your present mystical journey, and your future destiny can all be accessed on this inner plane.

The Wheel of Fortune meditation takes you to this Hall of Records, the Library of the Soul. You will visit this repository and open the book of your soul and receive the knowledge held secret until this point in your evolution.

The Library of the Soul

Perform your relaxation and breathing exercises. Call upon your spiritual guide. Experience its presence as you did in The Hermit meditation. Feel a sense of expansion or other awareness that signals that you are in the presence of your Higher Self. A flash of light, an energy shift, a body sensation, or a specific sound will help you know that your spirit or Inner Guide is present.

Ask to be guided to the Akashic temple, whose exterior features two sphinxes that signify wisdom and mystery. Allow time to get a sense of this temple's feeling. If you are ready, you will experience an energy shift, receive a vision, or hear sounds, attunements, or chanting. Note how you experience this temple, for you may visit it many times.

The jackal-headed Egyptian god Anubis, the guide of the soul through the inner regions, greets you. He will take you to the

Library of the Soul and the Hall of Records. Note the library; you can also come back here many times.

When you are ready, ask Anubis and your guide to locate your book of destiny. It may appear as a scroll or book. It contains knowledge about your soul. Focus on the book or scroll as it is placed before you. See your name printed upon it. You may see something other than your given name if you are known by another name in the inner planes, and you can ask for your inner-plane name to be revealed.

Ask to be shown this current incarnation's destiny. Your book opens, revealing both positive and negative. Ask to be shown positive destiny—an image, word, phrase, or knowing may come to you. It may appear on the page, or within your mind's eye. You may have an overwhelming sense of certainty about a heartfelt purpose, or hear words of power and comfort. Behold your greatest good and the grandeur of destiny's intent. Don't worry if you can't read or comprehend the information consciously; your subconscious and super-conscious will give you the information over time in the way that is most suitable for you.

Request to know your soul's purpose, gifts of the spirit, talents, and empowerment, and the meaning of your life, your karmic lessons, and your dharma or blessings and grace. Deeper understanding regarding a life challenge, especially a repetitive issue, is also available by turning to the life-lesson pages in the book. Know that what the negative pages reveal are the lessons and challenges your soul chose to learn; you can ask for clearer understanding. If you have discord and lack in your life, this is precisely where you can carry a lesson of cause and effect. Asking to be shown these pages will help neutralize the condition.

You can rewrite your destiny through choice. Simply visualize a fresh page or scroll; this may appear as white light. Write your desire, aspiration, or affirmation in the light, using a blue, gold, or orange light. Your writing is a demonstration of your choice to utilize free will to create your own effects by activating cause. The cyclical law will then be put into effect.

It is completely unethical to write the destiny of other people into your own. However, in some of the books, you may find the answer to questions you have regarding your destiny's link to another individual and the karma and dharma involved in that relationship. This will be revealed only if you are ready and sincerely seek to understand this lesson. Remember, not everything is meant to be known and not all things have been written; we have free will.

Turn to your Inner Guide for help or clarification, and to request any further guidance before exiting the temple. Afterward, your guide will lead you out of the Hall, and Anubis will escort you to the door of the temple. You will find yourself outside, then back in your waking, rational mind, fully cognizant of your experience inside the Hall of Records.

Write down the information and your impressions and descriptions in your journal.

JUSTICE

For whatever a man soweth, that he shall also reap.
(GALATIANS CH. VI, V. 7)

Pallas Athena, the goddess of Justice, is depicted on the Justice Arcanum. The ancients regarded her as the wise counselor in times of peace and the warrior's call to arms during times of injustice and upheaval. Known as both the Maiden Warrior and Athena, patroness of Athens, she governed over the preservation of spiritual societal ideals, independence, justice, righteousness, heroism, literacy, and wisdom through balanced divine and natural orders.

This goddess presides over the unwavering law of cause and effect, or karma, and bestows the blessings of dharma. Her divine law includes the potential for you to interact with her as an initiate. Pallas Athena serves the highest good, and, to that end, she offers you the opportunity to redress imbalances that are unjust by collaborating with her to deactivate those karmic conditions.

Interpretation

Behavior in word and deed based on soul truth; treating yourself with fairness, self-worth, unconditional love, and self-respect—integrity. A deepened awareness regarding your relationship to your gifts, powers, and aptitudes. A firm "knowing" concerning the good you have to offer and the desired contribution you feel destined to make to society or your sphere of influence.

Self-knowledge. Increased awareness of karmic responsibility and themes from this and other lifetimes. Stay mindful that you are part of a larger scheme involving an adjustment between your personal world and your destiny or karma. Refinement, serenity; flow of life circumstances that foster and support the fulfillment of positive karmic destiny.

Equitable, right, or fair choice-making in alignment with the wisdom and well-being of a harmonization between body, mind, and spirit. A sharp mind, discriminating and focused; clear perceptions; fair and just. The law of karma—i.e., action and reaction—is activated. Reaping what has been sown; conscientious sowing of correct intent in order to reap appropriate rewards.

Protection of the sacred authority; justice and righteousness will be served. Favorable legal outcomes. Humanitarian rights and social equality; legislative and judicial forces will help you.

Meditate on the Justice Arcanum to steady yourself in the face of disharmony and when faced with an injustice. Bring the actual card with you to important life situations when you need reason, independence, intuition, strategy, and adept management in negotiations and important communications that produce fair, honest, outcomes. Pallas Athena will ensure that justice is successfully served.

Reversed meaning: Life's circumstance force you to examine what has been ignored or remains unfinished in your evolutionary quest, and then action is taken. The area or aspect of your life that is in conflict, disharmony, repetitive cycle, or inertia is an exacting spiritual lesson. Turn to the Justice meditation for help correcting and redressing imbalances. Injustice. When this Arcanum shows reversed, you are often wondering whether you are being treated with prejudice. This card's reversal strongly indicates a prejudicial, negative situation, sometimes meaning that you may be treating yourself with cruelty, malice, and unfairness. Inability to choose education or career direction. A life path, schooling, or career choice is unrewarding.

Questions to Consider

- What do I need to integrate in order to balance my life?

- What is my subconscious prompting and prodding me to explore?

- Are my actions honorable?

- Can I allow myself to ask for and act toward acquisition of what I want?

- Do I act in alliance with my beliefs and intentions?

- Do I give as much as I get in return?

- Do I give excessively and disallow receiving?

Affirmations

I affirm my acceptance of spiritual, societal, and personal responsibility.

My negative karma is neutralized and rectified through adjustment.

I sow desirable seeds and stand open and ready to receive results within the rhythm of cosmic time.

Meditation

The purpose of the Justice meditation is karmic adjustment. This unique practice will help you acquire a highly refined equilibrium through elimination of that which produces turmoil. Justice helps you face your dis-ease, then wields her powerful sword to sever the ties that restrict. Your request for the severance from all unnecessary ties and bonds to a specific person, belief, or situation—bonds that may be hindering your peace and progression—is granted in this meditation.

Use the worksheet at the end of this section (see page 186) as a guideline during the practice. Have someone read the meditation to you, or record it and play it back.

The Karmic Adjustment meditation gives you a technique that enables you to neutralize old karmic patterns, release them, and heal the past. I liken this karmic adjustment to a cosmic version of the familiar chiropractic adjustments.

Karmic Adjustment

Start your meditation with an intention to address a serious imbalance, lack, or need—a chronic disharmony or residue from a deed in the past that needs releasing and subsequent adjustment; conflict regarding your will and the will of another person; extreme attachment to past conditions of disappointment, pain, or trauma; injurious personal belief systems inflicted directly or indirectly by another person or outside condition. All these conditions can be neutralized.

Your intention regarding the severance or adjustment is crucial. The law of karma will not fail; it will reveal your real motivation through the outcome of your actions and what you'll receive. Therefore, ensure that your intentions have integrity. Do not proceed with this meditation until you feel your heart's intentions are sincere and that you truly desire the severance of the ties and can accept the beneficence that will come to you.

Place the Justice card in front of you. Begin with relaxation and rhythmic breathing. Ask your spiritual guide or Higher Self to come into your energy field. Continue to breathe, relax, and expand your consciousness until your can sense its presence with love and clarity. Your guide, the presence of your Higher Self, will remain with you as you place a white light of protection around yourself and its emanation.

When you are ready, ask to be taken to the Temple of Karma. Enter. The interior floor has a black-and-white checkerboard pattern with gray stone walls. At the end of the hall are two gray pillars, two stairs, and a stone square. A violet curtain is drawn between the two pillars; a yellow light shines behind it. Approach the dais and stand in front of it. State your intention—that you have entered this holy place because you desire to sever the ties that bind you to a person, memory (this-life or past-life), or an unbalanced condition. Make only one request at a time.

Petition the Goddess of Justice for her help by standing before her stone cube and asking her to appear to hear and judge your request. She enters and takes form. Sense how she feels; note her sword and scales. You may look at your Justice Tarot card during this time, and it may change or you may feel its energy.

First, ask that the severance be to the good of all and the harm of none. Then name the circumstance, belief, negative behavior, or person. If you don't know the particulars, simply name the feeling and visualize a shape to represent it. You will not ask for an individual to be severed, only the unhealthy ties that bind. You can use the same method for any situation or an unproductive behavior, unhealthy belief, or negative feeling that can be visualized as an energy form, or simply felt or named, and completely severed.

The Justice figure will nod or otherwise inform you that you may proceed. She knows the karmic lesson behind the issue and will allow the request if it is karmically appropriate. Continue by sensing or visualizing the person, feeling, or circumstance standing before Justice, facing you. Ask again that the unproductive bonds and ties be severed to the good of all and the harm of none.

A very large sword of light, crystal, or steel descends with its point down and its handle up, decisively cutting the bonds. At first, you may feel a tugging or awareness of energy between you and the energy form being released. Note where you sense it, because that may be an area where you are vulnerable and tend to give energy away. You can correct this by sending white light to the area. Feel your energy return and watch the other's do the same. You may feel this as waves or currents, or experience it as streams of light.

Surround the form with a capsule or box of white light; seal it perfectly, then dissolve it in the light.

Turn back to the Lady of Justice; you can request understanding as well as assurance that all the bonds and residue have been dissolved. Ask her for guidance concerning any action you will need to take to reinforce the procedure, as well as insight concerning affirmation and visualization that will heal and harmonize. You can request deeper understanding regarding the karmic lesson of the matter so as to release beliefs that are associated to the condition.

Call upon your Higher Power, through a request or affirmation, to act on your behalf for the manifestation of your new healthy desire. Know that the law of dharma (joy and bliss) is available after the rectification of a past deed occurs. Imagine a set of balanced scales; focus your attention on them. See one of the pans filled with an image representing your hopes for your future, while inside the other rests a feather to represent truth. Surround the image with white light, then send out the energy within the image. Repeat your prayer or affirmation, especially emphasizing the statement of your true empowered intention.

Visualize, or actually extend, your arms in an open-armed gesture to form a scale, first moving, then coming to rest. We all desire peace in our lives and the mercy to be released from deprivation, pain, and suffering. Affirm that you are in peaceful alignment. Maintain your focus on the scales for a few minutes, then slowly prepare to close the meditation.

The scales and figure of Justice will begin to recede when the session has concluded. Ask your guide to escort you from the Hall. Once outside, feel your breathing return to normal and note your body and surroundings. Slowly move out of the meditation position and record your experience in the journal pages provided for you.

Karmic Adjustment Worksheet

Date:_____

_____

Time: _____

Perform the meditation from this section and use the outline below to record your experience.

I. Hall of Karma

Description:_____

_____

_____

_____

Felt like: _____

_____

_____

_____

_____

_____

2. Intention: (Purpose for my visit)

_____

_____

_____

3. Goddess of Justice appeared and felt like:

_____

_____

_____

4. Name the particular circumstance:

_____

_____

_____

5 Allowed to proceed: Yes _____   No _____

6. Experienced:

_____

_____

_____

During visualization, energy cord or bond location:

_____

_____

_____

7. Sword description:

_____

_____

_____

Successful severance (i.e., sword uplifted, scales balanced):

_____

_____

_____

8. Energy returned to me and felt like:

_____

_____

_____

9. Action needed to reinforce severance:

_____

_____

_____

10. Understanding as to why the condition existed:

_____

_____

_____

11. My dharma and joy for the future is:

_____

_____

_____

Understand that you cannot change the past, but you can make an empowered choice to refuse to offer more energy to a past memory. You are seeking a disconnection through this severance, then a healing, and finally an awareness and choice that there is a holier, more sacred, intent in which to place your energy.

You may experience a test after this meditation. The person or situation it targets may become a challenge; be aware and have a plan of action based on peace and integrity in place. After the test, you may sense that the attraction of the circumstance is no longer occurring, signaling your success. If you are attracted to, or continue to attract, the same situation, you may need to repeat the meditation.

Remember, always sever the bond and place the other person or situation in the divine light of the Higher Self. It is the light that knows how to heal the karmic connection for both you and the other. Most important, know that you are not in this life to be someone else's victim or a victim of the past, or a disempowered version of yourself. You deserve peace and now know how to attain it to the good of all and the harm of none. You are incarnated to fulfill the expression of your Highest Good.

THE HANGED MAN

Deep peace of the running wave to you.
Deep peace of the flowing air to you.
Deep peace of the quiet earth to you.
Deep peace of the shining stars to you.
Deep peace of the gentle night to you.
Moon and Stars pour their healing light on to you.
Deep peace of the Light of the World to you.
(GAELIC BLESSING)

The Hanged Man is often perceived as a card of suffering, but actually represents a lesson regarding its termination. He appears in a state of grace, symbolizing his true meaning, that of unity with the Divine. As The Hanged Man remains in the stillness of the spiritual center, his desires (which cause suffering from your attachment to them) cease because he receives complete fulfillment from the source that cannot fail.

I often refer to The Hanged Man as the "cosmic exchange department." The card represents a choice to sacrifice a lesser ego-based need in favor of a greater, holistic desire and peace. The word sacrifice means "to make sacred." The desire is made sacred by its elevation to its highest impulse.

The sacrifice suggested in The Hanged Man is that of the lower ego's desires. The only thing lost is the perception of neediness and a false sense of lack that is the original source of the suffering. Once centered in the Higher Self, Spirit is placed at the core of your being. Then all will be added on to you.

Interpretation

Faith replaces fear. Reversal of priorities. That which was once the ego's primary value and focus becomes unimportant. A new, evolved holistic viewpoint takes precedence over old, stagnant conditions. Replacement of the lesser ego and narrowness with a greater expansive life in the Spirit. Surrender of a limiting belief that prevents you from life fulfillment. The dissolution of the ego and pain caused by attachments. Falseness ends. Separation from the Divine ceases.

Reinventing yourself based on choices of self-love; allowing a more pure heart and identification with centering on a spiritual self into your life.

Renunciation. Baptism. Sanctification of life. Centeredness and remembrance of the infinite essence within each moment. The spiritual faculty attributed to The Hanged Man is stillness of mind chatter—the state of samadhi or union with God. It is a capacity to enter a deep state of meditation, directly focus on a question, and then receive guidance and information.

Reversed meaning: "Let go and let God" concerning the question. Surrender emotionalism and the need to be in control; correct whatever the ego perceives it needs, including victimization, perfectionism, power, and selfish grasping at others. Be "in the moment."

Remember your divine self and the immovable central core of your being. Keep your dignity. Align with that which fosters your union with your Higher Power.

Avoid reactionary behavior. Stand still. Practice detachment. Stop trying, forcing, and pushing. This stance encourages helping forces to come forward—forces that your focused type of "doing," "making," and "getting" mentality has not called upon or realized. Be open to receive from the higher planes through alignment of affirmation, prayer, and meditation, and asking for guidance. Tend to your inner life; take time to reflect on your dreams, daydreams, and inner dialogue through journal writing.

Relinquish the expectation of your desires—fulfillment on your timing or in the way you think they should come to fruition.

Give up unrealistic expectations of self and others. Cease controlling, especially when your actions are based on fear, insecurity, and deep lack of faith in your own goodness and deservedness, and the love of God toward you.

This card's reversal can indicate an addiction to suffering, and especially to victimization. Sometimes it represents an unconscious masochism and a deeply ingrained belief that the area in question will always be and always has been in a state of "lack." Another tendency with The Hanged Man reversed is that of the sacrificial victim—someone who is always putting others first, tending to others' needs, or "rescuing" others; a "missionary-like" tendency, a "carrying of the cross," codependence, or a long-suffering stance. You are not a victim unless you choose to be. Surrender your suffering; choose self-love; detach from dependency and fear-based possessiveness.

Questions to Consider

- What belief is fostering a struggle in my life?

- Why do I like to suffer regarding this issue?

- How does it make me feel like a victim, or otherwise reinforce old, negative beliefs?

- How can I act rather than react in my situation?

- What attachment to belief do I need to surrender?

- What needs to be dissolved, rejected, let go of, banished, or released?

- What would the opposite stance and thinking be like?

- How would it better serve me?

- How can I incorporate it into my affirmation, and then into my life?

- Where do I receive support? From my connection to the Divine, which always sustains me? Or from the

uncertainty derived from emotional and mental life
and the external world of people and personalities?
From illusion and delusion?

Affirmations

I am immersed in the One Self that is eternal.

I stabilize my personal world by detaching from my ego.

*Here in this moment I Am the manifestation of the infinite essence
within me.*

I Am the Great I AM in this moment.

*All situations are simply God's action to increase my learning and
understanding.*

I am willing and able to sacrifice the lesser for the greater.

I seek inspiration, not exasperation!

I am aspiration.

I am at peace.

Meditation

The meditation for The Hanged Man offers the powerful experience of letting go of the lower desires and their attachments that
produce trouble and suffering. You'll discover a way to relinquish
and dissolve your worries and your ego issues so that your heart
and mind become tranquil. This state promotes firsthand spiritual
experiences, miracles, and grace.

The purpose of the meditation is to offer up a problem or
personal suffering to the God of your own understanding. Surren-
dering false thoughts, attachment to suffering, and limiting ways
of perceiving life neutralizes pain and creates alignment with true
stability and an opening toward fulfillment. When you become

addicted to your adversity and perceived limitations, you need to seek, sincerely and with all your heart and mind, to understand the lesson brought to you through it. Then move on. To sacrifice a lower attachment, to surrender it, is to make your life more sacred in accordance with divine light, life, and love.

Are you the victim? Do you need to be superior? In control? Is your trouble caused by mistrust, fear, bitterness, inferiority, bossiness, insecurity? All of these beliefs can be renounced. Give yourself some time to define the precise issue that needs to be renounced. The sacrifice of the small, personal ego allows you to gain the greater, spiritual you.

Letting Go and Letting God

Begin your meditation with the usual relaxation and rhythmic breathing. Imagine your entire head surrounded with a white-light aura, as illustrated in The Hanged Man. Allow this light to become strong and intense; note how it makes you feel.

See the image that represents your struggle or unwanted attachment. It may be an event, a word, a self-image. See it floating out of the top of your head; then see it dissolve into the light. Ask that this issue's energy be dissolved and removed from your body, mind, and soul. See or sense it dissolve in the light again. A feeling or thought, as well as surprise about where you store issues, may be revealed to you. Now you know where you store other issues that can also be released through this new technique.

Affirm that you have "let go and let God" regarding this matter, which is now in the Higher Power's hands. Do not dwell on it, try to make things happen, or worry about it, because, if your ego gets involved, it will muddy the channel of faith that has been opened. Use a prayer or affirmation that fills you with serenity and reflects the divine impulse—love, abundance, spiritual awareness, or wisdom. Be open to receive the results with faith, balance, and clarity. Then trust in the Higher Power's timing; continue to keep the problem or request in the Higher Power's hands.

DEATH

Death is the veil which those who live call life. They sleep, and it is lifted.
(PERCY SHELLEY, *PROMETHEUS UNBOUND*)

The Death trump is known as The Lord of the Gates of Death and Child of the Great Transformers. The idea of transformation is key to understanding the true significance of this card. It represents metamorphosis and indicates a permanent desirable change from a lesser to a greater state of love and fulfillment.

The skeleton in the card represents the basic or fundamental human structure stripped to its bare bones. Now the solar or soul self can build a new entity upon this foundation. The animated skeleton moves toward the sunrise to symbolize the rebirth into the light body and a reorientation of life toward Spirit or Divinity.

The Death trump relates to the esoteric symbol of the phoenix rising from the ashes, having survived and been transformed. It also denotes the snake shedding its skin. The images refer to the liberation, regeneration, and permanent change of the emotions and personality.

Interpretation

The Death card represents liberation from the past. Personal regeneration and rebirth into spiritual wholeness are indicated. Death of an old unproductive aspect of the ego facilitates the birth of the awakened true self.

Your will has become aligned with that which serves the "good" in you. Your emotions are purified. Wholeness in alignment with your genuine feelings is restored. You are no longer attached to destructive immature ego behavior and fearful desires.

A permanent change occurs—a major transition from old to new, always for the better. The external reflects the internal, creating a move in location, vocation, or orientation. Life is undergoing a dismantling, a deconstruction, a decomposition, and reconstruction. It is time to choose a new plan, to say good-bye to the past, and move on.

Reversed meaning: Stagnant conditions occur through an inability to release the past. Change is sure to come. The release of unhealthy attachments is necessary to create this change. Unconscious of the power of choice, you remain in an immovable position.

Questions to Consider

- How can I be more productive and nurture what is already emerging in my life?

- In what do I have faith and how do I adhere to that faith?

- How does my imagination reflect my desires?

- What outworn, destructive thoughts, feelings, and behaviors need to cease so new ones can be created that are closer to my own desires?

Affirmations

My soul is a divine spark burning within me. It ignites and kindles the seeds of my spiritual potential.

My soul is in God's hands. God's blessings are in mine.

I align with God's intention to bring me into greater expression of my true self.

I release my dependence on the outside world. I tend to the great I AM within me and rest in faith that all will be well.

Meditation

The Death meditation is designed for you to experience the liberating energy of the Death card directly. This is a powerful meditation. It reflects the directness involved with complete change, the Death card's essential meaning.

Dying to Live Again

As you contemplate this card, imagine yourself in a scenic river valley waiting for the sunrise. You have complete faith that the Sun will rise as you face east. Your mind and body become acutely sensitive to the river's current. You feel it as if it were your own blood's flow. You sense its magnetic presence flowing from west to east to meet the sunrise. Feel the breeze as the branches of the trees rustle.

A sense of anticipation grows. You begin to feel and see the glow of dawn. A scent of roses fills the air. The sky turns blood red, then crimson, then pink. Then you see the gold orb of the Sun. Where do you experience this vision? Do you feel it in your head, your heart, or your entire being? Do you feel it with bodily sensation? Do you see it? Do you hear it?

The Sun directs a ray right toward you. Where does the ray go? Does it direct itself toward your feet? Your heart? Your head? Notice how you receive it. Are you open and welcoming? Do you feel afraid? Nervous?

As you enjoy the Sun's friendship, you hear the flapping of a ship's sails. Then there is another similar sound. This time, it is the flapping of a flag accompanied by a horse's hooves clattering on the ground. An armored skeleton on horseback approaches. He dismounts and stands in front of you. He is animated and purposeful. He exclaims: "All that are born must die. All that die must be born." What do you wish to have die in your personality? What do you no longer need as part of your psyche? This must happen to make room for the larger life in the Spirit. Name an aspect of yourself, a quality or belief that you no longer want or need, and speak it aloud.

Next, decide what it is that you wish to have born in your life. What character quality or characteristic do you wish to bring into being that will produce the effect you desire in your life? Speak it aloud.

"Consider it done," the armored skeleton exclaims. He holds out his hand. Inside it is a seed. He hands this seed to you. Take the seed and place it inside your heart or head. By the time you have accomplished this, he has vanished. The Sun is now high in the heavens, and you have begun the birthing process for a new, positive aspect of yourself.

TEMPERANCE

The best and safest thing is to keep a balance in your life, acknowledge
the great powers around us and in us. If you can do that, and live that way,
you are really a wise man.
(EURIPIDES)

The Hebrew letter that corresponds to the Temperance card is Samekh, which means a "tent peg" or "prop," or "to support and establish in strength." While we are like tent dwellers in life, moving from one place, dream, person, or situation to another, the strength of our inner spiritual connection never fails us. It serves as a strong anchor in the changing sea of life.

The Archangel Michael is the central figure in the Temperance card. His mightiness comes from his solar qualities of pure love and light. He invites you to forge a personal relationship with him by blending your transformed nature, achieved in the Death trump, with his divine presence. Temperance represents the spiritual experience of fusing the personal and angelic that produces the direct descent of the divine power into the tangible world.

Interpretation

The appearance of the Archangel Michael means that life circumstances are requiring you to "walk your talk"; a test of character, courage, or faith is presented. As you persevere, remember to call upon your spiritual guardian, represented by him, for fortitude balanced with behavior modification in response to the test. Act as he would; be self-loving, have faith, and stay dedicated to your personal truth. If you treat yourself and your situation as you'd want to be treated, profound transformation and great healing will occur.

When the Temperance card appears, teaching, healing, artistic creations, and gifts of the Spirit are indicated. This card represents the art of living.

Adapt your temperament to allow beneficial beliefs, habits, and behaviors into your life. This involves stretching self-perception and strength of character to include new ideas. You may discover that you are more than you ever dreamed. With patience and effort and continued mindfulness of the spiritual beliefs that foster inspiration with divinity, you can establish a happy and self-balanced life.

Take heroic actions if necessary to champion over negativity and to create a personality fused with self-love and faith. The mightiness of Archangel Michael promises strength and protection through adversity.

Reversed meaning: The Temperance card reversed indicates imbalance, extremism, lack of caution, addiction, and bad chemistry regarding situations or medications. You may be dealing with a situation that results from a too-hot or too-cold point of view. In other words, you may be overreacting or underreacting. There may be either too much energy, as in hyperactivity, and/or depleted, low energy and burnout. An uncompromising stance may leave you out in the cold and feeling vulnerable. Failure regarding tests of character and tests in general; you may have lost your balance. A lack of flow between personal and higher worlds is indicated.

Questions to Consider

- How can I infuse my authentic spiritual nature into everything about me?

- How can I reconcile my true self and spiritual essence with my daily life?

- How can I rectify my past so as to keep flowing with my present?

- How am I feeling tested and how can faith, hope, and charity help me balance?

- Am I tending to my healing?

- What does the art of living mean to me?

- How can I adjust and harmonize with my current situation?

- How do I offer service to those in need?

Affirmations

I am in conversation with my holy guardian angel.

My personal world is an expression of universal forces and laws.

I am perfectly protected in the power of God's light and love.

My Higher Self is within me and directs me at all times.

I serve humanity from the divine will emanating through me.

Meditation

The purpose of the Temperance meditation is to mix personal and spiritual energies to open the channel between heaven and Earth. The complete change that occurred in the Death trump paves the way for the spiritual light to take on a new form within the human vehicle. As this fusion occurs, your gifts of the Spirit will flower, and the seeds of your spiritual nature will bloom. Your life and personality will modify to facilitate their expression. The Fool's journey to know his spiritual nature has been fully realized.

Receiving the Light of the Spirit

Begin the practice seated comfortably; breathe and relax as usual. Place your palms together, facing and touching each other. Focus on your left hand. Experience and sense the energy within it. Proceed slowly, paying careful attention to your left arm, your torso, your leg, your foot, and then up to your neck and head. Sense the energy as you proceed, returning finally to your left hand. Repeat with your right side, noting any differences between sides. Focus back to the center, where your two palms are facing each other. Mix the energy within your hands and your entire body from side to side.

If your right side feels dull or stagnant, you may have difficulty sending or transmitting energy. Sometimes, this translates into an inability to ask for help or to give help to others.

If your left side seems stagnant or dull, it means that you have a block around receiving information. You may have difficulty accepting help from others.

Practice this energy-mixing to establish a balance between transmission (radiating, emanating) and receptivity (openness, sensitivity to incoming telepathic, empathetic information). The practice creates a balanced energy that the Higher Self and spiritual entities utilize for healing and activation of intuitive talents and gifts of the Spirit. The technique also opens the channel to Inner Guidance and the transmission of divine knowledge.

THE MAJOR ARCANA
15–21

C hapter nine features the series of Major Arcana that represent the humanized version of the spiritual experience.

THE DEVIL

*How art thou fallen from Heaven, O day star son of morning. How art thou
cut down to the ground, which didst weaken the nation.*
(ISAIAH 14:12)

The Devil corresponds to Lucifer, the
brightest angel in the firmament. Lucifer
became mistakenly identified with Satan,
the fallen angel, due to faulty translations
of texts in the Middle Ages. His legend
then became one of prideful rebellion
against God that resulted in expulsion
from Heaven. It is fitting that confusion
and mistakes are associated with Lucifer,
since this is the Devil card's mundane
meaning.

The trump represents the part of
you that has fallen into the darkness of
ignorance. It signifies the initial stage

of awareness regarding a break with Divinity (often described as unhappiness) and the life lesson that will eventually prompt a return to the light.

The Arcanum's secret correspondence is to the Black Sun, force of the Lord of Death or Hidden One, whose brother was the Sun or the Lord of Light. The Black Sun goes into the underworld, or darkness, to acquire a greater understanding of those nether regions and levels of unconscious. In some ways, he is more knowledgeable and wiser than his brother of light, the Archangel Michael featured in Temperance, because he is more familiar with the lower side of humanity. Note how the two archangels appear together in our Tarot sequence as Major Arcanum numbers fourteen and fifteen.

Interpretation

When the Devil card appears, your fears are dominating the situation. What you are running from is running you. The card indicates mistaken beliefs in the lack of the flow of love, abundance, spiritual power, and self-approval. The seven deadly sins of pride, avarice, lechery, anger, gluttony, envy, and sloth are the results of putting your faith in a disempowered version of life.

The trump represents an error in judgment. Fear and negative beliefs separate you from happiness and fulfillment. Be careful not to give away your power to other people and surrender your values to your fears, guilt, addictions, or shame. A negative past overshadows the present.

The Devil's appearance usually indicates a personal power leakage; this is characterized by a sense of feeling stuck, being haunted by the past, and by repetitive life situations. The problem and solution are internal, but need illumination. In this stage, you may be unable to face the truth. Look for cards that indicate realizations—the Aces of Cups, Wands, and Swords; The Star; Judgement; and The Sun. Conversely, if there are many card reversals—The Hanged Man, The High Priestess, The Empress, The Magician, or The Emperor—or negative cards, or The Moon, then the time isn't ripe for awakening. The best you can do is plant seeds of awareness without the expectation of a quick result.

You may be unaware of the belief that underlies your unhappiness, or be unable to face it squarely, producing the "elephant in the living room" syndrome in which everyone sees the problem except you.

The obsession with materialism, power, and appearance that enslaves you is a misunderstanding of desire and personal empowerment. This card represents the lower self that causes fear and pain. It tricks you into harmful thoughts and encourages you to behave in dishonorable ways. You may be experiencing self-imposed limitations and need to liberate the false aspects of yourself in order to empower your life. When you liberate yourself from these illusions, you can laugh, releasing the attachment to what you once held as valued.

Reversed meaning: Liberation from fears and limitations. Lessons have been learned and self-awareness increases. More personal power is experienced. Karmic lessons are learned and integrated.

Questions to Consider

- What enslaves me? To whom or to what am I in bondage?

- What false image do I worship? Youth? Glamour? Power?

- Do I imagine myself in fearful, impoverished, or otherwise distorted, mistaken images?

- What image truly represents my individuality?

- What did I have to repress to become socially acceptable? What does this lost self have to say to me?

- What character traits did I construct to protect myself from my original pain?

- What was my original pain?

- What coping mechanisms did I develop to survive?

- What are the lies I have been telling myself? Where do they come from?

- Does my fear of the discomfort of self-knowing prevent me from manifesting my true destiny?

- Do I see myself as a child of God, loved and protected?

- Can I stop blaming others and empower myself?

- What do I find blameworthy in others? How do these traits reflect my own hidden self?

- What aspect of life preoccupies me? Why do I avoid a closer look?

- Who or what do I seek to control because, in reality, this very aspect controls me?

Affirmations

I am a child of God. I am loved, protected, and enveloped in white light.

I act in true accordance with what the Divine wants for me.

I am in perfect alignment with abundance. I flow with spiritual illumination.

I call upon the Archangels Raphael, Michael, Gabriel, and Uriel to protect me.

Meditation

The purpose of The Devil meditation is to begin the process of soul reclamation through clarification of perception. Begin by simply observing how you interpret your experiences, since this is a reflection of your inner reality. Examine your view of the world and how this serves you or does you a disservice. You can use the question section to analyze you worldview. Do not judge; simply resolve to make more honest choices.

Creation of a productive perspective based upon faith and the connection with God's abundance is possible. The Devil meditation, Washing Your Eyes with Light, will help you eliminate attachment to fearful, false, or negative unconscious beliefs. This will enable you to perceive true power clearly.

Washing Your Eyes with Light

Begin the meditation with an intention—a specific prayer, affirmation, or simple request for illumination from your Higher Self or Inner Guide about an area of your life where you feel stuck, fearful, or otherwise challenged. Another option that is very powerful is to ask a question like: What am I not seeing?

Perform the relaxation and breathing exercise. This meditation practice is performed with open eyes. Visualize white light vibrating, radiating, beaming, or pulsing at the top of your head and imagine the crown of your head softening and opening. Turn your eyes upward as far as you can. Sense the white light descending from your crown like a beam into the space between your eyes. Move your eyes to focus normally and gaze ahead. Feel your eyes being washed in this clear, white light. This purifies the ego and lower emotions of fear and anger. It clears your vision so you can truly see as an innocent child sees.

Perform this simple meditation for five to ten minutes. The following days will bring new thoughts, productive ideas that haven't been fully realized, and inspired problem-solving attitudes and decisions. As the blinders are removed, your life will evolve toward authentic empowerment.

In The Devil meditation, you do not make judgments. You simply invite pure spiritual awareness directly into your life, for the seed of Spirit is the light-bearing quality that will serve your highest good.

THE TOWER

The Lord is my goodness and my fortress; my high tower and my deliverer.
(PSALMS 144:2)

Humankind's tendency to construct defensive walls of isolation based on fear (a negative aspect of the Tower card) was the theme of an artist's portrayal of The Tower at the Tarot exhibition in Ferrara, Italy. Two televisions were placed on two stacks of bricks. On each TV screen, a person appeared. They faced each other and began to speak; the discussion escalated into anger. As the argument intensified, bricks began to fall in front of each person's face, until so many bricks had fallen that a wall had been built and they could not see each other or be seen! They had become isolated, and a foundation had been laid for misunderstanding, escalating to anger and fear. This is the basis for most battles and wars.

The wake-up call is the blessing bestowed upon the walled-up characters in the trump. Spiritual truth directly strikes them, creating a great leveling; they are blasted from their position. The realization that we have a spiritual nature that can respond to God's vibration is the awakening experienced in The Tower card. We come to understand that we truly are linked to Divinity and that all humanity is also connected to the same source.

Ancient civilizations regarded lightning as a supernatural force. In the Tower card, it symbolizes the dismantling of limiting beliefs, a deconstruction and personal recognition of the power of the connection between the human and divine realms. The scene's illustration features a sky filled with a lightning bolt and fiery sparks. The heavens are active, and celestial clouds representing the spiritual mysteries appear.

Interpretation

Absolute truth wins out. An uncomfortable truth replaces a comfortable lie. Blessed liberation from falseness that imprisons. The "wake-up" call, an intense awakening and unsettling liberation from imprisoning circumstances, occurs. False beliefs, limiting conditions, restrictions based on fears, and closed-mindedness or closed hearts in oneself or others have reached a crisis. Tearing down of artifice; exposure, painful deliverance.

Selfishness, self-deception, and misunderstanding of power creates catastrophe. Shock, rude awakening. Upset due to sudden and unexpected upheaval and tumult.

Fallibility, culpability, prideful errors. Ignorance, a false sense of security. Shake up of the status quo; power figures fall from lofty unreachable heights. Often appears in power and hierarchical situations where demotions, firing, takeovers, and downsizing or resignation shifts the balance of power.

Fireworks, explosions, exposure, and expulsions. "Let go and let God"; personal will and ego have no power at this time. Emotional change, new stance; dramatic and assertive action based on truthful realizations and revelations. A turning point and watershed experience. New realization of who you truly are facilitates the recognition of limited, erroneous beliefs.

Reversed meaning: Same as upright, but the disaster or change is known and anticipated. Spiritual interpretation same as above, but a more gentle energy awakening uproots stagnation and offers up energy to be willed and directed toward more empowering, true, authentic desires.

Questions to Consider

- During a tumultuous period in my life, how did I survive? What can I use from that experience to help navigate current circumstances?

- How does speaking out or speaking up for myself feel to me?

- What happened in my childhood and adolescence when I spoke my opinion, objected, or could not speak due to punishment? Was I unheard? Punished? Hurt? Betrayed? How does this affect my owning and embodying my own desires today?

- What do I need to feel safe to speak?

- Is it okay to "go for" the desires I deeply have and deserve?

- Do I really know what I want and do I have the courage to marshal my resources and dedicate my will to this objective? If not, why not?

- Remember a situation that brought a "wake-up call." In retrospect, was the truth liberating? Did it bring you freedom?

Affirmations

I am in alignment with and rely upon the divine will and its divine plan for me.

I open my crown chakra to receive the full illumination of the light of the God force.

I affirm awakening to who I truly am.

Meditation

The characters in the card are blasted from the fortress of isolation. Perhaps they are the prisoners depicted as slaves in the prior Devil card. The purpose of The Tower meditation is to free this inner prisoner. The practice is designed to help you confront and emancipate yourself from an imprisoning belief.

Choose an area of your life where you feel as if you are being held prisoner. We can be held captive by false beliefs, the past, and other people's needs. The symptoms are a sense of limitation and a struggle to gain freedom. Another way to understand this is as a feeling of being blocked. This presents itself in your life as an area that frustrates or disempowers you. The issue may be internal—for example, an inability to ask for what is needed—or external—relationship challenges, career restriction, or financial barriers that prevent the manifestation of your true desires.

Freeing Your Inner Prisoner

Decide the area you would like to work on and write it down so you can be crystal clear about the life areas you want to release. Seat yourself comfortably with your spine straight, or stand. Breathe deeply and rhythmically, moving light and energy up and down your spinal column. Breathe and energize your spine from bottom to top for one to three minutes. When you are ready, ask your Higher Power or Inner Guide to come forth. This is your source of protection and enlightenment; feel its warmth surrounding you. Allow ample time for this to occur fully.

When you are ready, call forth the "block"; see it as one of the prisoners who falls from The Tower. Imagine the character that represents the problem standing in front of you. Sense, see, or hear its presence. Now ask it what it believes—how it feels about the issue you have decided to face. It may change shape. You may hear a voice speaking words that haunt you or you may have a feeling that reminds you of an experience. Be vigilant to recognize the voice, feeling, image—whatever and however you are shown.

Now tell the image that its belief is false and does not serve the best in you. Tell it that you and your Higher Power intend to dissolve it with the white light of purification. It may fight back.

Again, heed what it says or how it behaves; this may surprise you. A hostile reaction as a control mechanism is standard. It may threaten, distract, or feel upset because it perceives itself as vital to your protection from harm.

Picture a pure white beam of light completely surrounding the character. Ask your Higher Power to heal, enlighten, and transform it, and then watch the miraculous transformation. It may disappear, because it has completely outworn its purpose. Or it may evolve into a completely different positive figure, an ally. For example, the harsh angry woman you've seen as The Tower card's female figure may transform into The Empress or the Queen of Cups. The insipid weak male figure may become the Page of Pentacles, a part of you that is open to new learning. The figure or the energy that shapes it becomes your spiritual ally and has vital guidance to offer you. Through meditation or journal writing, you can access this new knowledge. If the figure refuses to transform, use the white light to dissolve it completely.

You can use this meditation to liberate yourself from beliefs and programming that have created limitations for a variety of issues in your life. The power to choose and to take action is the liberating, positive facet of The Tower—the great triumph of liberating truth.

THE STAR

Where a spring rises or water flows there ought we to build altars
and offer sacrifices.
(SENECA)

THE STAR.

The Star represents the inspired manifestation of the true self. The beauty of the authentic nature is uncovered. The character on the card has become one with the flow of divinely guided expression of her unique brilliance.

Isis Urania, the goddess in the card, balances between the cosmic waters and nature. She recycles energies from the unrefined to the refined, Earth to heaven, natural to celestial, in service to a greater good of the human spirit. The pouring of the vases represents anointing and consecration, reception of divine grace, prophecy, gifts of the Spirit, and service to humanity. These gifts are shared, and it is through the giving that she continues to receive.

Interpretation

The Star represents renewal, healing, brilliance, holistic integration, empowerment, acceptance, and the true heart's desire. You are in the process of developing your own individuality, genuine talents, unique gifts, and aptitudes. Promising and inspiring motivational conditions that are in alignment with your soul purpose are successfully expressed.

This is a good time to befriend yourself and to be sincere and honest in dealing with yourself and others. Self-acceptance, self-respect, and self-worth are very important now. Develop your aptitudes and listen to the prompting of your Inner Guide.

The Star indicates the practice of meditation that helps establish a partnership with the metaphysical self and restore inner and outer harmony. As this occurs, new motivational inspiration provides hope and true happiness.

The aspect of true friendship is highlighted when the Star card appears. You may be giving encouragement and love to or receiving encouragement and love from a friend. A soul mate is involved with the question. The soul mate experience can happen more than once in a lifetime. A beloved, a child, a parent, a family member, a kindred spirit, a muse, or a friend may be a soul mate, making an evolutionary contribution to your life and vice versa.

Reversed meaning: The Star card reversed indicates despair, energy blockages, and depression. There is a disconnection from life flow and a lack of self-love and self-worth. You may be demonstrating an inability to embrace your gifts, talents, and authentic self. You may be uninspired, unquestioning, and unable to act in your own best interests.

Questions to Consider

- Have I been tending to my chakra meditations, purifications, and visualizations?

- Have I been contemplating, asking questions, and unearthing my own answers and spiritual potentials through this process?

- Do I believe in healing my traumas so as to recycle stuck energy toward my highest good?

- Do I have faith in evolving my own psyche?

- Have I been acting as my own best friend?

- Have I endeavored to be a loving support to my friends?

- Do I allow my friends to support and uplift me?

- Am I involved with a group of like-minded people?
  Do I need to be in such a group?

Affirmations

These affirmations are based on the seven chakras. See the meditation for more discussion of the chakras and their meanings.

First chakra (base of spine): From the root of my being, I am fully incarnated and grounded; I treasure my connection with nature. I walk my talk.

Second chakra (navel/pelvis): I am expressing my sexuality with love toward myself and my partner. I love and honor my gender and sexual nature with sacredness.

Third chakra (solar plexus): I take my power back from any individual, prior experience, or past life. I own my own power from this day forward.

Fourth chakra (heart): I love myself. I respect myself. I deserve. I am loving compassion.

Fifth chakra (throat): I speak my truth and confidently claim I only allow individuals in my life that are healthy for me to experience. I am a cocreator with Divinity.

Sixth chakra (brow): I listen to and seek guidance from my intuition. I open and vitalize my relationship with my psychic faculties through my will and the power of light.

Seventh chakra (crown of head): I experience Divinity in my conscious and subconscious being. I know my angelic/cosmic self.

Meditation

The stars in The Star card represent the chakras. The stars of the Pleiades, Venus's seven handmaidens who offer spiritual gifts, are also symbolized, since these gifts are also associated with the chakras. The lotus flower also symbolizes the chakras, as do wheels of light and pools of spiraling energies.

There are seven subtle energy centers, or chakras, located in your etheric energy body. Your etheric body exists directly next to your physical body and intermingles with it. It is seen as a fine cloud or mist-like energy around the physical and works with prana energy, chi, and breath. Your etheric body channels vital energy into, around, and out of your physical body.

The chakras are described as two-inch energy disks that slowly revolve or pulse. They can appear or be felt as vibrant spirals or radiating Sun-like energy. Energy is channeled from higher spiritual levels into your physical body through the chakras. You then express that energy on the Earth plane. In other words, you ground the current and become the embodiment of the Infinite expressing itself through humanity.

Emphasis on chakra awakening, purification, and alignment helps you attain direct spiritual awareness through entrance into the higher worlds through the opened crown chakra.

Following is a brief summary of the seven chakras and their meanings.

First chakra (base of spine): Represents grounding, the ability to manifest, the capacity to understand where true support comes from, and the ability to feel that life and nature support survival. It is involved in past-life recall, soul mates, reincarnation, and karma. The color associated with the first chakra is red.

Second chakra (navel/pelvis): Represents reproduction and creative supportive relationships. Sensuality, confidence, a state of well-being, and the capacity to give and receive pleasure are centered here. Astral projection is associated with the second chakra. The color connected with the second chakra is orange.

Third chakra (solar plexus): Represents empowerment, a sense of strength and willpower to stay strong and honorable and true to yourself. It is associated with creating reality, mind over matter, thought forms, synchronicity, dreaming, and the ability to act on intuition and belief. The color associated with the third chakra is yellow.

Fourth chakra (heart): Represents the feeling of loving compassion toward oneself and others, as well as unconditional love and forgiveness, self-love, acceptance of others' struggles, and noninterference. All types of healing are represented, as is the ability to effect positive transformation. The colors associated with the fourth chakra are pink, green, and gold.

Fifth chakra (throat): Represents speaking your own truth, having your own voice, and a feeling of being heard. There is a capacity to speak with clarity and genuineness. Spiritual aspects include telepathy, sending and receiving messages, and cosmic truth. The color associated with the fifth chakra is blue-green.

Sixth chakra (brow): Represents the ability to heed intuition, the sensing and experiencing of spiritual guidance, visions. Divination, clairvoyance, clairaudience, universal love, and compassion are all connected to this chakra. The colors associated with the sixth chakra are violet and indigo.

Seventh chakra (crown): Represents the capacity to commune with divine energies and understand your God potential in a personal, functional way. It is involved with cosmic consciousness, union, bliss states, and the spiritual flow in daily life. Mediumship and channeling are connected to this chakra. The colors associated with the seventh chakra are red-violet, violet-white, and crystal.

Aligning Your Chakras

Seat yourself in a comfortable position; perform your rhythmic breathing. Feel yourself grounded and relaxed. Focus your consciousness at the base of your spine by imagining your energy traveling to that location, or by actually moving your attention into the first chakra. You can place your hands at the base of your spine to help you focus. Breathe into that center.

Feel the energy pulsing, moving, and circulating. If it feels blocked or sluggish, picture a slow whirlpool movement in that region, a pulse or a heartbeat. Sometimes, if the chakra is vibrant or ready to open, the energy will expand, and you will feel it become larger. Experience each chakra by imagining it opening as a lotus flower opens. Close the chakra by closing the lotus.

Imagine a red lotus flower opening its petals or a wheel of red light spinning. Extend this to your feet and down into the core of the Earth. Say aloud or silently speak the affirmation: "I am connected to the present moment. I feel life's energy and vitality coursing though my body."

Move your consciousness to your pelvic region and the second chakra. This center of reproduction, creativity, and sexuality is pulsed with an orange color. Experience the same lotus or wheel as you did for the first chakra. As you breathe and surround this area with the orange energy, you may feel like rocking or gyrating your pelvis. This is a sign that the chakra is functioning and becoming free. Repeat the affirmation: "I love and accept my creative nature. I express my sexuality in sacredness and conscious, loving choice."

Next, move to the third chakra, located in your navel region. The yellow color of this center relates to the idea of the Sun and is a power generator. Focus here when you desire to feel strong and centered in your own power. Experience a sense of beaming, radiant energy. This center gives you permission to be your real self. The affirmations are: "I express my true will. My power is the servant of the light."

Focus on the fourth chakra, the heart center. You cannot fully experience the blessings of the higher centers unless your heart is opened. The heart chakra transforms passion into compassion and generates unconditional love toward self and others. Visualize a green or pink light and coordinate this light with your heartbeat. Inside this chakra is a deity of loving compassion. It may present itself to you as a spiritual character, a saint, or a Buddha seated upon a lotus. The affirmations are: "I am love. I express the universal will to love."

The fifth chakra is a power point for contact with spiritual truths and systems of universal understanding. When you feel comfortable expressing your own truth and can hear others' truths with objectivity and intuition, this center is functioning harmoniously. This center initiates a creative approach to life. When seeking successful communication with others, the muse, inspiration, and creative genius focus on this center. Repeat the affirmation: "I honor my own opinions and express myself with creativity and clarity."

The sixth chakra, or third eye, is located above the bridge of your nose. Focus your attention on the point inside your head where light beams from your eyes and ears would intersect. Spend a few minutes experiencing this convergence. As you do, visualize a white moonlit sphere the size of a dime. This is your pituitary gland. Psychic faculties are located in the sixth chakra. Multidimensional awareness—communication with your Inner Guide, or with spirits or angels—as well as the psychic faculties are experienced from this chakra. Repeat the affirmation: "I am in perfect reception to intuitive awareness and honor my visions, intuitions, and spiritual self. My prayers, affirmations, and visualizations are in perfect harmony with the universal laws."

The seventh chakra corresponds to the pineal gland in the center of your head. Often symbolized by a pinecone, a thousand-petaled lotus, a crown, or a halo, it connects with cosmic consciousness and the divine emanation of God. The crown chakra is a place of contact with spiritual beings and their powers. It helps when you focus on this center to imagine the crown of your head softening. This allows for a freer circulation of energy into and out of the chakra. Sense the center as a vibrating white or crystalline light descending into the other six chakras like a beam. Now move more deeply into the light, becoming its thousand-petaled lotus. This is often accompanied by an altered state of serenity, splendor, and unity.

You are now the light and energy of the chakras. Feel each one and the pulsation and radiance of each of their individual vibrations. To finish the meditation, imagine each one closing as a flower would. Start from the crown and work down to the base of your spine.

Afterward, you may feel moved to partake in a tranquil activity. This is appropriate and advised. Continue to tune into your body during the activity; it may be subtly reacting to your meditation. Where and how may show that you need to focus more on the particular energy pattern and chakra or chakras involved. Simply breathe into the energy; it will naturally reveal its message to you.

THE MOON

The night brings counsel. When deep sleep falleth upon men, in slumbering upon the bed then He openeth the ears of men and sealeth their instruction, that He may withdraw man from his purpose and hide pride from man.
(JOB 33:15)

The Moon represents the sensitivity and subtlety of emotion, psyche, and psychic impressions that inhabit your inner world. She governs memory, childhood, mothering, the feminine, the waters of life, the unconscious mind, the night mysteries, and the ancient and primeval self. The path to reclaim the unconscious self through a mystical nonlinear path is illustrated in the card.

The psychic aspect of the body mysteries are represented by the Moon Arcanum. The Star represents the chakra system, the conduit to the spiritual realms housed within the body. The Moon symbolizes the body-chemistry mysteries involved with the glands, specifically those allocated to the chakras that govern psychic activity—the pineal and pituitary glands—as well as the solar plexus. Visceral and vital, their energies are familiar to you as the magnetism used in natural healing power. Among the qualities allocated to The Moon are instinctive psychic faculties like intuitive dreams that reveal mystical information and uncover past lives, and experiences in which you predict the future or visit with those in the afterlife and telepathically communicate to other times, places, and people.

The Moon is known as the card that represents the reorganization or adaptation of instincts in preparation for holiness. It relates to awakening, purification, and alignment between spirit, psyche, and body. Adaptation of your body chemistry, lifestyle, habits, tastes, desires, and dreams occurs as negative emotions are cleansed. Self-awareness increases in preparation for a happy, spiritualized life. Occultism teaches that, during sleep, the brain, involuntary body functions, cell structure, blood chemistry, and glands are all affected by the image you have of yourself. Through holding a positive heartfelt image of yourself, you impress these organs and functions, and in turn, they become imbued with the image through a kind of holographic effect. Magnetism then attracts the external conditions that reflect this image to you. The purification concept associated with the Moon card is another way to develop spiritually, to rise up (the Moon rising) to the highest image and aspiration possible. In time, your entire body system will reflect this spiritual growth on a physical level.

Interpretation

Psychic impressions, future forecasts, accurate predictions, and correct insightful intuitions are represented by The Moon when it is surrounded by positive cards. The High Priestess, The World, The Hanged Man, The Lovers, Temperance, The Chariot, Aces, Queens, Pages, and Knights are all optimistic, helpful cards that indicate a constructive interpretation for The Moon.

Powerful dream messages are occurring. Consult a good dream-interpretation book, visit a dream analyst, or speak with an expert about the material.

The challenging aspects of The Moon will be indicated if it is surrounded by the above-mentioned cards reversed, The Devil, or other negative cards. Some of the trials indicated are a feeling that personal energy has been drained by someone, the carrying of an emotion that belongs to another, a sense of invasion, imbalance, or vulnerability, poor health habits, and loss of connection to everyday life. Delusion, confusion, addictions, victimization, and deception of self or others are indicated.

Take the time to analyze the invasive feelings. Ask yourself if the mood is really your own, or if you have been invaded by someone who doesn't take emotional responsibility for his or her own feelings. When does this occur and around whom? Does this remind you of another time in your life? The opened psychic self that goes unprotected, and therefore vulnerable, can be remedied. Visit a spiritual healer, and practice protection techniques that you know to help stabilize yourself. When new balance has been reached, the other problems will no longer be attracted to you.

Reversed meaning: Improved conditions are indicated. Revelations of truth; clarity yields positive action. Adjustments are made and there is calm and restoration of balance. Love and truth are stronger than confusion and deception. Adaptation of lifestyle and energies to incorporate psychic and spiritual aspects is evident. A deepened understanding of metaphysical powers, laws, and principles are utilized to your advantage.

Questions to Consider

- What are my night dreams telling me?

- What am I hiding from others or from myself?

- What emotional cycles keep repeating in my life and what does this say about me?

- On what issues do I need clarity?

- What bodily symptoms—e.g., cravings, weaknesses, addictions, and stress reactions—do I repeat? What are they trying to tell me?

- How can I be more receptive in my life? How can I change, allow myself to open, and receive genuine help from others? How can I open to receive help from spiritual sources?

- What conditions do I need to establish in order to allow change and receptivity to occur? Do I need solitude, guidance, pressure, support, analysis, structures, deadlines, a mission statement, or a program or plan?

Affirmations

I imagine myself into being.

I am holy. My body, soul, heart, and mind are holy.

I sanctify every atom, molecule, and cell of my being.

My body is a temple of God.

Meditation

The meditation for The Moon is an astral-scan technique. It will protect you and purify your energy field as you venture into these realms.

Scanning Your Astral Body

This practice requires at least a half hour of undisturbed privacy. Begin by relaxing from feet to head, breathing rhythmically from your diaphragm.

Focus your attention on the top of your head. Imagine a white light beaming out of the top of your head. Now take a stream of this light, like a band or a beam, and pour or send it very slowly down the front of you, as if you were scanning your body from head to toe with your hand. When you have finished the first scan, return to your head and repeat the scan slowly down a different part of your body.

As you proceed with your scan, you may become aware of an energy shift, like a hot or cold spot. You may find yourself inexplicably blocked when you reach a certain part of your body. When this happens, ask for information. An image, memory, feeling, or other awareness may surface. There may be a lack of energy flow in this area. It may feel uneven, inappropriate, very hot or very cold. You can dissolve this energy block by pouring more white light into it to release it and restore balance.

Repeat the scanning beams, moving from head to toe and then returning each time to your head.

This is a lesson in working with astral light, energy currents, and magnetism. You attract what you believe. You magnetize certain conditions for good or ill into your energy field based on your history and beliefs. Now that you know how to clear and smooth your energy field, you can do so on a regular basis. This helps the new, positive programming within your cells and psyche create a holographic effect for your entire being. That magnetism will attract happy, beneficial soul-power experiences for your progression.

The undulating path illustrated in The Moon card represents how soul progression occurs—through ups and downs, dips and curves. It is not linear or within the control of the ego. It enlightens, then seems to disappear. It is changeable, sometimes available and sometimes not. The ever-changing Moon symbolizes how the journey functions. Meanwhile, spiritual adaptation, represented by the wolf and dog, is occurring secretly.

THE SUN

When I was 42 years and 7 months old, a burning light of tremendous
brightness coming from heaven poured into my entire mind, like a flame that does
not burn but enkindles. It inflamed my entire heart and breast like the sun
that warms an object with its rays. All at once I was able to taste of the
understanding of books—the psalter, the Evangelists and the books
of the Old and New Testaments.
(HILDEGARD VON BINGEN)

Many cultures throughout history wor-
shipped the Sun because of its power to
destroy darkness. Its ever-present all-giving
warmth symbolizes the unfailing certainty
of Divinity.

A theme of rising, raised, or arisen is illustrated in The Sun card. The child depicted is
lifted up to an honored status, symbolized by
the crowning and the seat of honor astride a
horse. The flag is raised, the sunflowers raise
their heads to face the child or son, and the
radiant Sun rises without fail.

In astrology, your Sun sign—the zodiac
sign under which you were born—shows who or what you're in
the process of becoming in this incarnation. It characterizes your
essential self, personal power, honors, recognition, self-confidence,
success, joy, and healing, as well as leadership, natural energy, standing firmly in your true power, growth, mastery, truth, and independence. The double appearance of the Sun and the son in the card
points to the two levels in the zodiac for each sign—the usual and
the spiritual, or raised, version.

In a reading, when the card that represents your zodiac sign
appears with The Sun card, the higher attributes of the sign to help
encourage and guide you are emphasized. For example, if you are
an Aquarius and The Star card appears, emphasize meditation and

alignment with your highest personal truth for guidance. The following are the masterful, higher expressions attributed to each Sun sign:

Aries: Insight, reason, intellect, and will under the dominion of the Higher Self.
Tarot card: The Emperor.
Message: Envision and build your entire life on a foundation of wisdom and spiritual love.

Taurus: Intuition, inner teachings.
Tarot card: The Hierophant.
Message: Listen to your inner promptings. Develop trust with your Higher Self through meditation or prayer.

Gemini: Discrimination and discernment of the Spirit, healing.
Tarot card: The Lovers.
Message: You can sense spiritual energy and presences. You can also heal others and yourself using spiritual sources.

Cancer: Creative word, magical speech.
Tarot card: The Chariot.
Message: Your life will magically transform through the speaking of your own truth. The creative power of your voice and your ability to express your essential nature is transformational for you.

Leo: Transformed heart, love.
Tarot card: Strength.
Message: Your compassionate heart is your strength; it will give you abundant love.

Virgo: Wisdom, attainment of soul power.
Tarot card: The Hermit.
Message: Trust your wisdom; it will help and guide you and other people.

Libra: Equilibrium, laws of cause and effect.
         Tarot card: Justice.
         Message: Act and react from the center of your highest truth and you will have balance and peace.

Scorpio: Regeneration, mystical occult powers.
         Tarot card: Death.
         Message: You have the ability to improve your life by raising your aspirations to their highest potential.

Sagittarius: Art, spiritual zeal, and intensity.
         Tarot card: Temperance.
         Message: Embrace your aspirations with zeal and you will attain inspiration and reward.

Capricorn: Renewal, empowerment through understanding the misuse of power and instincts.
         Tarot card: The Devil.
         Message: You will renew your life through faith and service to a Higher Power.

Aquarius: Meditation, inspirational consciousness.
         Tarot card: The Star.
         Message: Meditate. Channel your entire being into your natural talents. Follow your inspirational star.

Pisces: Trance, bliss.
         Tarot card: The Moon.
         Message: Eliminate anything unworthy of your sacred self; live in conscious union with spirituality.

Interpretation

The Sun symbolizes direct, conscious cognition of the spiritual energies of divine love, truth, harmony, and wisdom. This joyful, light-filled awareness enlightens the body, mind, and spirit. The power of radiance and the heat of the Sun toward the everyday world and humankind are central to your survival, creating a metaphor for your relationship to God and the divine will.

The Sun represents qualities of joy, self-expression, healing, protection, growth, and blooming of the heart's desires. It signifies birth and the simplification of life. Its arrival in a spread marks the beginning of the creative, intuitive, authentic self—free, liberated to express its "God-given" potential. You may be realizing true love, happiness, and the development of positive committed relationships. The Sun card represents marriage, independence, empowerment, healing, mastery of education, and consciousness-raising.

This card can symbolize the appearance of an enlightened master, a spiritual teacher, or a healer who offers illumination.

The Sun signifies the harnessing of the will toward a particular goal. The ego is now in service to the Higher Self's divine plan, which, in turn, creates the energy to provide you with balance, stability, and protection. You have overcome the darker aspects of the soul and consciousness; clarity and wisdom reign. Do not to keep your "light under a bushel."

Reversed meaning: There is an inability to devote your life, mind, and heart to service of the Higher Self. You are closed to healing and wisdom, preferring darkness over light. Negative unconscious thoughts and beliefs hold your will captive, and you are unable to see clearly how to make changes in your life.

Questions to Consider

- What aspects of my life bring me happiness and joy?

- When do I feel complete and comfortable, and sense the natural flow of life?

- Do I feel comfortable and positive expressing my unique talents, will, and thoughts?

- What kind of energy do I radiate to others? Is it peaceful? Provocative? Vulnerable or negative? Angry or judgmental? How does the energy coming back to me from others reflect what I am sending outward?

Affirmations

I am a child of God.

I love my strengths and seek to raise them to their highest expression.

I express love that is pure, noble, and wise.

My will is directed toward divine glory.

I serve the spirit of light in all I say and do.

I ask for and receive gentleness, harmony, prosperity, love, health, and wisdom from the power of the Sun.

Meditation

The words "Sun" and "soul" come from the same root. As you perform this meditation, your soul will become energized with radiance and your heart and mind will open to the flow of the divine. Perform this meditation outdoors, if possible. Watching the Sun through a window is also effective.

The Refiner's Fire of Purification

Relax your body and prepare for the meditation by taking some deep breaths. Close your eyes and face the Sun if possible. Imagine what it would feel like if you could gaze directly at the Sun. Take time to connect with its color, brilliance, and heat, and the power of its light.

Close your eyes and visualize the Sun drawing closer, until it is just outside your body, hovering at your heart area. See a path of light or ray beaming from the Sun toward your heart area. Now, very slowly, bring the Sun into your heart as you breathe in. Notice how it feels as you do this. Sense it shift your energy while you hold your breath. As you breathe out, visualize the Sun leaving your heart area and returning to a position just outside your body. Repeat this breathing in and out two more times, very slowly. Each time, it will feel different. The third time you do this breathing, the Sun may significantly increase in size or in sensation.

Repeat the three breaths again, this time shifting your focus to your diaphragm (solar plexus). Notice how it feels compared to your heart. Repeat the sequence three times at your brow.

As the meditation continues, your entire inner energy field will light up, creating a radiant full-body halo-like effect. Become aware of this and feel or visualize the light growing stronger, warmer, brighter, and purer. This is called the Refiner's Fire of Purification. It activates the authentic self and attracts beneficial experiences and people to you. It removes negativity and ensures protection.

Remain in this state for ten to fifteen minutes, then slowly close down your energy field by picturing the glowing orbs of the Sun becoming smaller—and placed inside your brow, heart, and solar plexus as if they were seeds. Focus on breathing normally and fully return to your usual waking consciousness.

You may discover subtle shifts in your energy and attitude, or in how other people respond to you as a result of this practice. Be mindful and attentive to your surroundings and dreams, for the Refiner's Fire will subtly adjust your life, creating beneficence.

JUDGEMENT

Just as there was only one at the beginning, so too in this work everything comes from One and returns to One. This is what is meant by the reverse transformation of the elements.
(SYNESIOS, FOURTH-CENTURY GREEK ALCHEMIST)

A mighty angel sounds a horn and a man, woman, and child are raised up by its vibration. The Archangel Gabriel is the source of this great awakening and call to reunion with him. Gabriel, known as the Strength of God and Archangel of the Spirit of Truth, is often depicted with the white Easter lily as a symbol of resurrection, annunciation, love, and revelation. Gabriel appeared to numerous illuminati of spiritual history, including the Virgin Mary, Daniel, Joan of Arc, and Mohammed.

The Judgement card illustrates a soul moment—the times in your life when you are moved by the spirit and feel a direct, unmistakable reunification with Divinity. A moving religious experience, encounters with the spiritual world, an answered prayer, and the witnessing of a spiritual being are some examples of the soul's vibration raised by and through a direct encounter with the divine world. When this happens, your physical, mental, and emotional bodies are united with the powerful soul energy and filled with spiritual love, wisdom, and knowledge. These are the moments when you know that something greater than yourself exists and works through you. When you recognize your soul's immortality, the outcome is often life-transforming, bringing great empowerment and healing.

Interpretation

The Judgement card represents triumphant announcements. A new addition to the family, a rite of passage, retirements, moves, life progressions, and accomplishments are indicated. An empowering career change or promotion is forecast. You are involved with circumstances that will benefit you. You are accepting your own power and are guided by your conscience.

A balanced loving supportive relationship of sustenance and acceptance with family members (biological or chosen) helps everyone be the best they can be. A discovery, creation, and bonding with a family of choice, those individuals with whom you share values, interests, and aspirations.

Judgement's appearance indicates an empowered connection to the essential, authentic self. It denotes a soulful time in your life, highlighted by a profound dawning of spirituality and recovery of life purpose and meaning. The ego-driven world becomes smaller, and limiting familial values recede while the soul purpose expands your life.

Ascendance over old conditions. A particular life cycle and soul lesson, no matter how difficult, is now understood from the vantage point of the spiritual journey. You no longer attract or need this lesson and can permanently move to higher ground. Resolution and release of troubling psychological issues, challenging behaviors, and detrimental family conditions. Peace and reunification with the soul and authentic self.

Reversed meaning: Inability to release the past. Family emotional patterns impede your growth. There is stagnation, a lack of love, and disempowerment. The Judgement card reversed indicates an inability to offer up the toxic self for cleansing and release, and to accept forgiveness and unconditional love. Unconscious beliefs and trans-generational family values require psychological attention.

Questions to Consider

- What is my soul's purpose?

- How am I fostering my soul's purpose?

- Do I love, accept, and forgive myself unconditionally?

- Do I understand that my soul's empowerment belongs to me, not others?

- Is it not my duty to place my relationship with my spiritual values above others' toxic needs, especially if it disempowers me?

- Do I understand that true power is derived from my soul's linking with the spiritual realms?

Affirmations

The foundation of my strength is God's infinite bounty of love.

The foundation of my being rests secure on the bedrock of my soul, my true being.

I purify and sanctify my entire being.

I am not my family. I am not my mother, my father, my ancestors, my children, or my loved one. I am not my body, my emotions, my thinking, my profession, or my worldly possessions. I am the essence of my soul in love with the Divine—the light, love, and wisdom that manifests through all I say and do.

I am free to express my soul's purpose.

Meditation

One of the gifts of this Arcanum is the full recognition of your divine purpose as something more than an abstract thought or wish. Your spirit's spark, first ignited in The Fool's heart, now fills your entire being and you feel connected to it.

The releasing of old personality traits takes place, and your life is liberated. This makes space for your true soul self to enter your entire life and transform it. Your transformed self has the capacity to honor the new direction as true and valid. The meditation focuses on preparing for this experience by releasing that which impedes you from this transformation.

The Judgement trump introduces the idea of trans-generational healing, because the card depicts the family unit raised to a healed, holistic reunion with the soul.

As your spiritual nature matures, your psychological programming and personal family will be affected internally and in reality through the power of vibration. It is at this time that you may become aware of family beliefs that are out of alignment with your soul truth. These are the attitudes and values, spoken or unspoken, that are typically of an emotional, reactionary nature.

By choosing to heal them through the Archangel Gabriel's power of love and release, you can enable yourself and your entire family to progress and heal the disempowerment. As the energy once held is expelled, a soul-power experience descends upon all involved. This is the experiential understanding that you all are connected and that the one affects all.

The theme of this meditation is the reclamation of the soul and its purpose through the releasing of psychological programming derived from faulty family precepts that do not serve your highest good. Family patterns are examined with the idea of keeping the best and releasing the rest.

You have the opportunity to heal negative beliefs, especially those handed down through the generations. As you neutralize the hindrances, the helpful qualities will arise and create empowerment.

If you have undergone comprehensive healing on a topic and it still has not been "fixed," use this meditation. It involves perceiving family and relationship "cords." These are energy cords or bonds between people. When they are negative in nature, they limit potentials and are constructed on unproductive beliefs. In other words, you wouldn't wear your grandfather's old worn-out ill-fitting coat, would you? Then why wear or carry his programming about life, money, or love when it is as poorly suited to you as the coat? Part of the empowerment represented by Judgement, along with the strength symbolized by Archangel Gabriel, is the bravery to make different empowering choices.

Trans-generational Healing

First define the belief that you wish to heal. Write it down and consider why you have this idea. Ask yourself, if it doesn't come from you, whom does it come from and when? And why? Family convictions are passed down from generation to generation. Sometimes all you need to know is the general idea behind the thinking so that it can be released.

Begin by visualizing the family member you sense has the belief you would like to release. Picture this person and their ancestors standing in front of you. See or sense the undesirable belief and the relationship cords between ancestors. You can also use an actual photograph of the person or persons.

Always ask your guide to connect with the other person's guide and request that the healing intention be for the highest good of all involved. Request that cooperation to deactivate and neutralize the relationship cord—again for the good of all and the harm of none—be granted by the spirits of all involved with the meditation. Your guide will inform you if you cannot proceed.

Focus on the belief represented and see all the generations that carried it. Visualize or sense the bonds dissolving into the ocean portrayed on the card. Then affirm that now those who carried them are relieved of their burden. Ask to go back to connect with and dissolve all the cords for as many generations as necessary to release the chosen conviction. Now ask that the belief cord be severed, neutralized, or released for the good of all and the harm of none.

You may experience resistance or confusion from the central person and all the prior generations. Simply send all of them white light and request a permanent release through Archangel Gabriel's power of divine love. See the relationship cord break. Use white light to dissolve the energy and ask that each member receive the healing light and love of the God of their own understanding. Allow ample time for the Archangel to heal the energies of all involved, including you.

Close the meditation by affirming a release of everything you have said and done to support this belief and then forgive yourself for supporting negative beliefs. Surround yourself with Gabriel's white light and affirm that you've taken back your power and that the new energy is dedicated to the awakened soul and its purpose.

Reunion with the soul elevates your heart, mind, and body, raising it to its spiritual potential, purpose, and highest good. When this happens, the spiritual family enters your life. Your family of origin may change, or you'll find a new family to which you belong. Remember that, since you are working from a spiritual perspective, the timing is that of the soul. Rest assured that, whenever you make these changes, it is appropriate. When anticipated shifts occur, it will be on the soul's schedule, not the ego's.

The World

Therefore we may consequently state that: this world is indeed a living being endowed with a soul and intelligence ... a single visible living entity containing all other living entities, which by their nature are all related.

(Plato, *Timaeus*)

The *Anima Mundi*, an androgynous figure also known as the world soul, is The World card's central figure. She represents the pure spiritual energy that permeates nature and animates all matter.

A mandorla-shaped wreath encloses the figure. The mandorla is an ancient, oval-shaped symbol used to close up something of great value, usually a religious figure, by surrounding it in a protected shield of light. The Anima Mundi and mandorla symbolism define the meaning of this card—that humankind can share in the nature of heaven; in becoming human, we can become divine.

The full development and display of our spiritual nature and the capacity to administer this energy is now "sealed" within the human potential. The crowning attainment of this evolutionary cycle has been achieved. The next stage is to return into the personal, everyday world as an emissary of light from the perspective of mastery, empowered with confidence and willing to share. The journey is completed and begun anew.

Interpretation

Mastery, successful results, positive completion of a cycle. Victorious expression of self-knowledge; responsibility and talents through a life path that furnishes reward and recognition in your chosen avocation. Embrace your excellence; success is yours and it is the time to share that which has been mastered. Expertise is rewarded.

Authority is well managed and maintained. The confident management of great resources and large endeavors is forecast. The authentic self achieves success and satisfaction and fulfills its contribution to the world. World travel may be indicated. Prayers are answered, and there is protection for all.

Cocreation with the cosmic blueprint, happiness derived from dancing to the music of the soul; your life is imbued with meaning. Destiny fulfilled. Soul purpose attained.

The World associates to divine movement practices like spiritual dance, meditation walks, yoga, Tai Chi, ritual, ceremony, performance art, Gaia studies, the connection with nature, and experiencing sacred places on the Earth.

A rewarding trip to a place that calls to your soul is another way to experience the Anima Mundi's sacred energies. Allow the vibration of the chosen location to move you and share its wisdom by being open to hear and respond.

Reversed meaning: The reversed meaning of The World is a success of a less profound nature. You may need to assess the accomplishment for areas where there is still a need for improvement.

Questions to Consider

- What does success mean to me and how am I fostering its manifestation in my life?

- What can I do, wear, or acquire that will symbolize my commitment to my intention and attainment?

- Do I believe I am worthy of success?

- Do I feel confident in the management of worldly and spiritual victories?

- Do I understand that I am the dancer embracing and performing the "dance of life"?

- Do I understand that masters guide me and that I am a manifestation of "as above, so below"?

- If I don't act and participate in my own unique expression, who will?

- How can I best express my expertise, authority, and wisdom for the benefit of others and myself?

Affirmations

I manage my success on all levels through God's grace.

I rest in knowing my intention, will, and imagination are fully dedicated to the embodiment of my true nature and purpose.

"As above, so below."

I am the expression of the divine will to good.

My father and I are one.

I dance myself into being.

I express and manifest excellence.

Meditation

The World meditation is based on envisioning the twenty-two Major Arcana surrounding you, as if each were a leaf in the mandorla wreath illustrated in the card. The practice features connecting with each Major Arcanum, then merging with each for integration and ending up releasing the energy to allow the next one to take its place. The ability to accomplish this requires a level of spiritual mastery, the ultimate meaning for this trump.

The ability to visualize all of the Major Arcana encircled about you simultaneously requires the concentrated focus of The Magician. You can place all the Major Arcana around you in sequence in an oval shape and turn to face each one as you engage and integrate, and then release them. The meditation should be performed standing if at all possible, because it requires movement.

The Wreath of Protection and Integration

Begin with your usual breathing and relaxation, then imagine yourself surrounded by a huge oval garland or victory wreath. Each leaf unfolds, becoming one of the Major Arcana in their natural sequence from zero to twenty-one. Allow ample time for this first step.

Then face each Arcanum. Feel its energy; see its light; sense its vibration; connect with it in whatever way you choose. The energy may communicate with you the way it chooses; be open and receptive. Make clear contact with it, then request it to merge with your energy. Note the shift; the archetype may have a message for you, therefore do not move quickly through this stage. When you feel sufficient time has passed, release the archetype by seeing or sensing it leave your energy field. Each Arcanum in turn moves forward, passing through you and out the other side.

Note that the quality that each card embodies is available to you. Now realize that you are not separated from these energies. You stand inside them, just as the Anima Mundi stands inside the mandorla wreath.

Then realize that you already are these twenty-two energies. Take ample time to realize this potent statement completely. Congratulations, you have attained a level of mastery.

PART FOUR

NEW MEANINGS & MEDITATIONS FOR THE MINOR ARCANA

In the next two chapters, we'll look at new divinatory and spiritual definitions for the Minor Arcana and Court cards. We'll learn stream-lined meanings for each card and explore meaning for challenging cards. You can add these meanings to your Tarot vocabulary to enhance your repertoire of card interpretations.

·10·

THE MINOR ARCANA
AND THE FOUR VIRTUES

The classic Four Cardinal Virtues of Courage, Faith, Justice and Charity take on fresh significance when applied to the four Tarot suits. The meanings simplify your interpretations and at the same time serve to spiritualize them. How empowering to hear that faith is the key to opening the heart (Cups); courage is the message for achieving your goals (Wands); your gifts and talents are the source of your riches (Pentacles); and that integrity means being true to yourself (Swords). The Virtues will give you interpretations of new depth and accuracy.

The streamlined attributes for the Minor Arcana are based on their original historical affiliation with the four virtues of fortitude, faith, justice, and charity. These correspondences date back to the Renaissance and the medieval eras. The interpretations will help you make sense of the cards by using one common theme that threads its way through the entire suit. The meanings are inspirational and uplifting, and provide guidance and predictive information. You'll quickly see how these new meanings apply to the cards and enrich your interpretations.

The four virtues correspond to the suits as follows:

Courage	Wands
Faith	Cups
Justice	Swords
Charity	Pentacles

When a Minor Arcanum is dignified—in other words, positive—
we will refer to it as a triumph. When it is not dignified, or negative,
we will refer to it as challenging. The triumphs are those cards that
represent the courageous successful expression of the authentic self,
as well as the fortitude to attain goals and achieve victory.

WANDS

Creative energy expressed through the will of the individual human
spirit is the theme of Wands. The Wand cards represent claiming
and celebrating your true place in the Sun. Without the virtue of
courage, none of the triumphs described in the suit can occur.

The original meaning ascribed to the Wand suit during the
Renaissance was fortitude, bravery, or courage. The fifteenth-
century peasant class was associated to Wands, and card illustrations show humble clothing and challenged behavior in the Five,
Seven, Nine, and Ten of the suit. The remaining cards, including
the Court cards, are characterizations of triumphs of the human
spirit. Successful people and endeavors are illustrated; the cards'
scenes are productive, and the costumes are regal and refined.

When a number of Wands appear in a reading, you are ambitious and filled with aspiration and enthusiasm, and have real
desires about your query. Be encouraged when you read these cards
and believe in your goals. Accept that you deserve the success and
accomplishment by treating the subject of your inquiry seriously.

The suit represents the equation "passion equals energy"; it
reflects doing what you truly want to do (not what you have to do).
When you are bravely aligned with your authentic self, your destiny will naturally unfold. Continue valiantly fueling your desire for
growth, because this is when real change, improvement, and happiness occur. Begin to claim and celebrate your true place in the Sun
fearlessly.

For example, when cards indicating the early part of your desire
or dream—the Page, Ace, Two, and Three of Wands appear—
know that all greatness begins with an idea, and that this idea is

both real and good and deserves the quality of daring determination. At this point, your desire may be in a vulnerable stage and need encouragement.

Be direct and honest, but gentle, when challenging cards like the Five, Seven, Nine, or Ten of Wands and reversed Court cards appear. You will need courage and fortitude to face these trials. A test requiring a defensive stance and self-assertion with clear intention is at hand. How do you intend to handle it? Define the tests or challenges and consider themes of Courage. Knowing this will help you clarify and prepare for what is ahead.

The Ten of Wands, a particularly challenging card, has a special meditation for consciousness-raising and problem-solving in the "Meditations for the Minor Arcana Challenge Cards" section on page 261.

Triumph Cards

The Wand triumph cards are the Ace, Two, Three, Four, Six, Eight, Page, Knight, Queen, and King.

Ace: Birth. Fearless expression of the authentic self. An auspicious, powerful idea comes to light; encourage its development.

Two: Boldly dedicated will and imagination wisely directed toward destined goals. Noble, sincere intentions attract beneficence.

Three: Courage, understanding, patience, and fortitude yield results. A project flourishes toward its destined conclusion or fulfillment.

Four: Courage, optimism, and determination result in fulfillment of a cherished goal. Embrace your triumphs and celebrate your victories.

Six: Heroism. Stand tall, as a shining example of leadership. Reward from well-balanced efforts.

Eight: Fearless, daring action channeled toward a goal. Determination produces quick results.

Page: Courageous authenticity. Let your true self shine.

Knight: Boldness, valiance, heroism. A triumphant winning of life's tournaments as part of the spiritual quest. Values of transformation and evolution.

Queen: The radiant heroine. A woman who thrives because she's found her true place in the Sun. Warmth, generosity, optimism; failure is impossible for her. Spiritual values.

King: Hero, determined leader. A man who is accomplished, warm, and generous. Courageous, fearless, and spiritually attuned. Strength derived from a clear moral compass.

Challenge Cards

The Wand challenge cards are the Five, Seven, Nine, and Ten.

Five: A challenge of courage involving speaking your truth and taking a stand. Test of determination balanced with adaptability and willingness to compromise. The positive value of competition.

Seven: A challenge of valiance and confrontation; heroic steadfast dedication to your goals and position. Ability to tackle the adversary bravely and give them "the boot."

Nine: A challenge to protect and safeguard your boundaries, dreams, aspirations, or position. Stamina, resilience, and steadfastness are the test. Preparedness is advised.

Ten: Resilience, endurance, and stamina are the qualities illustrated. A challenge to remove unnecessary burdens in your life fearlessly is the test. The Ten of Wands meditation on page 261 provides guidance and problem-solving techniques.

Reversed Wand Cards

In general, the reversed Wands indicate an inability to accomplish these tests and triumphs. Courage and determination is lacking, as well as vision and the ability to believe in your own potential. Encouragement, bravery, optimism, heroism, positive role models, and attaining rewards are the antidotes to the reversed cards. Highlight the idea of the human spirit and the power of self-determination to face the challenges posed by the ill-dignified cards.

CUPS

The virtues for the suit of Cups are faith and love. You will be reading about relationships with family, significant others, friends, lovers, self-love, and heartfelt endeavors. The soul self, subconscious, dreams, and spiritual, psychic, and meditative states that correlate to the virtue of faith are also represented. Other qualities associated with Cups are imagination (to image constructively or negatively) and creative ability.

This suit associates to the element of water and the sense of taste. It represents tasting life—the sweetness and bitterness of emotions and feelings, the saltwater tears of joy and grief, and the live-giving elixir and revitalization of soulful living. In each instance, openness to flowing with soulful and heartfelt feeling is essential.

Cups associate to being open, responsive, and able to flow with the feeling of heart and soul. The challenges therefore are stagnation, living without hope, mistrust, and disbelief. The meditation on page 263 for the Five of Cups, the challenge card of the suit, provides a fresh way to reconnect with belief and love by focusing on faith in the future.

The element of water suggests hidden depths and life's mysteries of love, soul, birth, caring, healing, and vision. Water's nature is constant yet cyclical, symbolized by the tide's relationship to the Moon and the certain crashing of the sea's waves in a rhythmic fashion onto the shore. This corresponds with the predictable ebb and flow involved with love mysteries, as well as the relationship of your soul's journey and your creativity. Sometimes it is low, at other times it is high. But it is always present.

The sacred cup or chalice symbolizes faith, initiation, baptism, and abundance, and represents the covenant between God and humanity. Ceremonial cups like the Holy Grail, symbolic of consecration, blood mysteries, and containment of the sacred aspects of life, are suggested in the Ace, Two, Four, Seven, Page, Knight, Queen, and King of this suit. Only those with perfect faith and a pure heart can glimpse the Grail. It makes sense that the Renaissance associated Cups with the clergy.

Faith is the historical virtue attributed to Cups. Faith opens your heart, and heals and renews the relationship with your creativity, soul, and loved ones. Each card of this suit has an attribute of belief ascribed to it, and the subsequent reversal or negative aspect can be interpreted, not only as loss of flow, but as loss of faith.

Triumph Cards

The Cups triumph cards are the Ace, Two, Three, Four, Six, Nine, Ten, Page, Knight, Queen, King.

Ace: Faith in miracles and direct communion with Divinity.

Two: Belief in the healing power of human love commingled with the soul and Divinity.

Three: Faith in life's natural flow of creative abundance. Loyalty and trust yield beneficence.

Four: Faith in spiritual guidance and vision. Assurance of soul message.

Six: Faith in devotion to the love of children, family, home, harmony, and peace creates a foundation of trust.

Nine: Confidence in prosperity and abundance shared.

Ten: Faith in spiritual blessings expressed as devotion and gratitude toward the beloved, family, and permanent partnerships yields fulfillment.

Page: Faith in mystical intuitions, dreams, visions, and soul-based messages. Belief in the muse and inspirational sources. Trust in the conception of creative ideas.

Knight: Dedication to the quest of the soul purpose. Belief in a higher calling; creative and mystical visions. Faith in the power of love.

Queen: Trust in divination and psychic revelations. Confidence in soul powers, vision, and metaphysical systems of awareness. Faith in the Tarot cards.

King: Trust in spiritual values and ethics. Dedication to faith in life's joyous possibilities expressed through the role of the initiator—i.e., educator, guide, creator, healer, visionary, or advisor.

Challenge Cards

The Cups challenge cards are the Five, Seven, and Eight.

Five: Faith tested; belief in the grieving process and in time healing; faith in the future. The meditation for the Five of Cups focuses on the challenge of releasing the past and opening to the promise of the faith-filled future.

Seven: Test of values; challenge to trust personal discernment and choice-making based on loyalty and commitment to the inspiration of the Higher Self.

Eight: Faith in the soul's quest and purpose; conviction toward walking an evolutionary path.

Reversed Cup Cards

Upright Cups indicate the ability to feel and flow with constructive emotion. These are not necessarily happy feelings, since the mourning and soul-searching, as seen in the Four, Five, Seven, and Eight of Cups, are also part of the emotional world.

Reversed Cup cards are characterized by reversal of flow or living in the past—regression, lack of flow, and emotions that are blocked, toxic, or torrential in their impact; conditions overwhelming and capsizing the situation or person. Feelings are buried or hidden. Problems with the ability to trust oneself or others, emotional manipulation; a closed heart and the inability to establish or maintain contact with genuine desires and feelings are associated to the upside-down Cups.

Often, reversals indicate losses concerning love and romance. Grieve, and release the pain in order to evolve and move beyond loss.

SWORDS

Justice and truth are the virtues for the suit of Swords. Uprightness and loyalty are qualities worthy of the dedication vowed to them by the historical knighthood classification assigned to this suit. The military, nobility, and aristocracy are also attributed to the Swords, as they have the power and position to uphold justice, integrity, and truth. These positive character traits connect to the Knight, Queen, and King of Swords. We also see this clear veracity in thought and deed in the Ace, Two, Four, and Six of Swords.

Another way to understand justice is the idea of integrity or righteousness defined as treating yourself as well as you would other people. Honor and fairness are the keys to understanding the strife depicted in some of the challenge cards. Treating yourself unjustly or lacking personal moral and spiritual integrity result in self-betrayal and harm to others. These are the negative psychological meanings of the Swords. Since this is the suit associated to action and mind, the healthy or troubled mental classification is appropriate. Doing the right thing by aligning with your personal truth, self-honoring, and treating yourself with integrity are the tests presented by the Five, Seven, Eight, Nine, and Ten of Swords.

The Sword suit of the Tarot is double-edged, signifying duality—help and hindrance, striking and cutting, and fighting for peace and ideals. Throughout history, there were consecrated Swords used in regalia and ritual, each indicative of conference of power. Their symbolic virtues and attributes are applied to the card meanings for deeper understanding of the specific powers of the suit.

Triumph Cards

The Sword triumph cards are the Ace, Two, Four, Six, Knight, Queen, and King.

Ace: The Sword of Spiritual Justice. Triumph over all obstacles. Peace reigns.

Two: The Sword of Peace. The triumphant alignment with personal integrity. Patience and serene waiting and reflection; to sit and "be" with the situation, allowing time to pass and changes to occur that reveal truth and correct decision-making information.

Four: The Sword of Religion. To bind back is the original root of the word "religion." The card features this principle with a prayerful knight reconnecting with his true source of power.

Six: The Sword of Mercy. A merciful benefactor has brought aid in the form of a guide and the power to move forward. Triumph of making honorable choices; dignity and fairness are the motivation for positive change.

Knight: The Sword of Curtana. This sword is used in ceremonies to confer knightly power. The Sword of Temporal Justice and Honor are given to the triumphant knight. Power balanced with integrity and righteousness is the basis for his swift actions and powerful intellect.

Queen: The Sword of Faith. Her life circumstances have taught her the triumphant development of great intellectual skills and a mind-over-matter attitude. Her faith in her Higher Power has sustained her, and she derives her power from this source.

King: The Sword of State. Triumphant in peace and war, the King possesses integrity, stature, and the power to make and keep justice.

Challenge Cards

The Sword challenge cards are the Three, Five, Seven, Eight, Nine, Ten, and Page.

Three: The challenge presented through sorrow and tending to a wound in need of healing. A test of compassion, understanding, suffering, repentance, or sacrifice is indicated. The Three of Swords meditation on page 265 will help you to heal the wound.

Five: A trial of integrity. Unjust and unfair treatment of self and others causes you to become a victim; you are defeated due to mistaken beliefs. The test is to recognize what is really desired or what is truly best for you; a clear definition of true values. The challenge is to walk away from negative, "no-win" situations.

Seven: A test of honor. The card represents a challenge to rectify unjust actions, dishonesty, betrayal, immorality, and unethical actions by aligning with truth and integrity. You are a victim of betrayal or your own self-betrayal, and the challenge is to become self-honoring in action and mind. The card's meditation on page 266 provides guidance on healing the betrayal aspect of the card. In other words, the wound is internal and external, and tending to one can heal the other. The attraction of the unjust foes and destructive conditions will cease after you use the practice.

Eight: Disempowerment due to injustice to self or interference from others. A challenge to ask for guidance and help for liberation from false perceptions; limited thinking and weakness is indicated. The Eight of Swords meditation on page 268 is designed to liberate your Inner Self.

Nine: Challenge of acceptance of loss, grieving, releasing, and forgiveness. The forgiving may be toward oneself, another person, or life's injustices. The test involves working through the loss to process it and move beyond it, rather than allow it to imprint itself upon you. This can result in the attraction of more of the same due to faulty beliefs, such as the loss was deserved or that the injustice will always be the theme of your life. A past pattern of sorrow derived from personal experience and family beliefs is released through the Nine of Swords meditation on page 271.

Ten: Challenge to accept a failure or ruination. The card can also represent a necessary release of energy held in a form, so that it can recycle into a better form. A test of faith in a Higher Power; belief that all energy doesn't die, it just takes another form; confidence that the end of the old brings birth of the new. Renewal and rebirth are positive themes in the card; if surrounded by good cards use this meaning. If surrounded by negative cards, the test of faith is indicated. Rely on the power of prayer, faith, and words of inspiration to ease the suffering. The Ten of Swords meditation on page 273 concentrates on the resurrection aspect of the card by focusing on the sunrise illustrated in the card.

Page: The card's meaning fluctuates. On the positive side, it represents a successful, adroit capacity to discuss, negotiate, debate, adapt, and interpret. A challenge to remain steadfast in action and thought that serves truthful and fair motivations is the test.

The meditations for the Three, Seven, Eight, Nine, and Ten of Swords feature renewal of hope derived from liberation from untruths, and a wholehearted acceptance of deservedness of integrity and justice.

Reversed Sword Cards

Dishonorable, dishonest, and harmful life circumstances that are unjust are the situational wounds that strike and cut. The Sword challenge cards and reversed cards indicate a split away from integrity resulting with injustice. Again, the choice of attitude and response is crucial. For the challenge to be met, you must determinedly "steel" yourself and muster the strength of character by fighting and winning battles. Meditations for facing and healing these wounds are featured for the Three, Seven, Nine, and Ten of Swords.

PENTACLES

The Renaissance and medieval eras associated Pentacles with the virtue of charity or benevolence. Charity, ultimately, is the giving of onself to God and is a noble quality. Striving to work with the charity God gives to humankind through the "God-given" gifts of our talents, capacities, and aptitudes is symbolically portrayed in the Pentacles suit. When you endeavor to labor lovingly with your gifts, you are cultivating a spirit-in-action relationship with Divinity.

The Pentacle symbol of a star within a circle represents a human being encircled by Spirit. The human is the five-pointed star, while the circle is a time-honored symbol of eternity and the divine realm. Gaze upon a Pentacle and you will discover that your eye continues to move around the image, suggesting an eternal, infinite relationship between the human and Divine.

This is the suit of wealth, and the idea of benevolent sharing. Values, valuables, and that which is deemed of worth are the practical aspect of the spiritual Pentacle theme. The characters labor lovingly for that which they value, whether it is family, prosperity, knowledge, or charity. Rest assured that the gifts from Divinity are being happily expressed. Generosity and the altruistic aspect of love shared with family and friends, and expressed in public service, faith, and social causes are the values portrayed. High regard for constancy and security in relationships, professions, and money is represented.

Pentacles represent the artisans, the crafts, and the merchants of the Renaissance world. Pentacles, Coins, or Disks correspond with the element of earth. Harmonious earth energy gives you abundance, stability, and security. Therefore many of the cards represent the securing, cultivation, and caretaking of your finances and resources. People who are happily aligned with their true calling, soul purpose, aspirations, and destiny are represented by the Pentacles. These people value constancy, productivity, practicality, perseverance, work, and faith.

Triumph Cards

The triumphant acquisition, management, and charitable sharing of resources are the theme for the Ace, Two, Three, Four, Six, Eight, Nine, and Ten of Pentacles, as well as for all the Court cards of the suit.

Ace: The charity of Divinity expressed toward humankind through the gifts by which you cultivate your security. Health, wealth, resources, talents, people, soul, and the inheritance of the Earth plane are represented. The card symbolizes the beginning of a labor of love in family, career, relationship, or spiritual growth that will triumph because it is sown, cultivated, and made manifest on good soil.

Two: An infinity symbol in the card reminds you that your resources are a gift from the Infinite Intelligence. Work with it to create a harmonious balance of spirit in action. Triumphant flow between the personal and universal forces establishes the ability to adapt masterfully to changing circumstances on the Earth plane. Success through understanding the infinity symbol's meaning of the law of cause and effect; giving and receiving in eternal harmonious balance.

Three: Triumph of masterfully crafting the spiritual, knowledgeable self. God-given gifts of abilities are mastered, attainment of honor and beneficial teachers.

Four: Powerful establishment of tangible resources. Triumphant management of material conditions.

Six: Known as alms with justice—a heartfelt sharing of resources with others. Charity and benevolence given to those in need.

Eight: Triumph of learning to work with talents and aptitudes. Lovingly laboring toward the learning, crafting, and development of a relationship between spirit and the personality self.

Nine: Triumphant cultivation of the gifts of the Spirit yield rich rewards of wisdom and full development of the communion between Spirit and humankind.

Ten: Triumphant establishment of spiritual and material inheritance. Beneficence expressed to family and loved ones. Rewarding capacity to express generosity with your gifts to others' benefit.

Page: Triumphant learning connected with gifts and aptitudes. The student labors lovingly at his educational goal.

Knight: The Knight's quest is to develop the gifts bestowed upon him. He knows this is his calling, values its meaning, and patiently endeavors to cultivate the practical and ethical qualities that will serve the manifestation of his powers.

Queen: A woman of means who is altruistic and generous, doing as she would be done by. She has her heart in the right place and is often involved with benevolence and charities. She has wisely developed her talents and seeks to help others make the most of their aptitudes.

King: Has developed and mastered his talents, creating industry and permanent, tangible, prosperous conditions. His labors and patience are also for love—his family and loved ones. He believes in doing as he would be done by and is altruistic toward others, even establishing charitable institutions and services.

Challenge Cards

The Five and Seven of the suit are the challenge cards. The test of value and worth is illustrated. The Five shows two indigent people in need of charity and the Seven represents a revaluation. The Five and Seven meditations address a need to reconnect with talents, riches, and charitable benevolence.

Five: Features uncharitable conditions. The characters need to ask for charity, as suggested by the lighted church window, symbolic of sustenance and light. The meditation for this card on page 274 tackles the subject of inner impoverishment, and that of emotional, mental, and soulful poverty and alienation.

Seven: Previously important endeavors have lost their value. An important revaluation is occurring. Encourage reflection and analysis. You may have outgrown or finished something once valued and your resources may have changed. Seek the cultivation of your special gifts.

Reversed Cards: The Pentacles challenges are those of uncharitable conditions both inwardly and outwardly, lack of value in work and profession, low self-valuing, belief in cruelty, and alienation from spiritual sources and creative gifts. The reversed cards show all these troubling conditions. Utilize the upright meanings for positive solutions and guidance.

• 11 •

MEDITATIONS FOR THE MINOR ARCANA CHALLENGE CARDS

Understanding challenging Tarot cards has always been daunting for interpreters. Here, we'll look at meditations that provide insight about the challenges depicted in the most troubling Minor Arcana. I've given problem-solving ideas and new realizations for each card.

TEN OF WANDS

Perform breathing and relaxation before starting your meditation. Imagine you are the character in the Ten of Wands, hunched over with your burden of obligations and responsibilities symbolized as the bundle of wands. Doesn't it feel strained, as if you could drop the bundle at any time? It isn't carried appropriately. It should be neatly bundled and on the character's back, using the back's natural strength, not carried on the front. Feel the strain and the weight of the wands in your arms. Feel how your vision is blocked. An  inability to imagine how to handle the responsibilities differently is also part of the problem.

Now see yourself slowly laying the bundle down. Stand up straight and stretch. Feel the release of tension and breathe deeply. Take time to examine the wands before you pick them up again. Are they really yours, or are some responsibilities and burdens being placed on you unfairly?

Ask the character in the card, or your Higher Self, to help you sort out what you really need to carry, what you can discard, and what you should tackle later. Concentrate on each of the ten wands and name each one. For example: career issues, expectations, health, relationships, past pain, inappropriate behavior from self and others, guilt, martyrdom. Place each wand in one of three piles—now, later, or discard. Can you see how your preoccupation with your burdens has kept hope, life, positive options, and helpful influences from your attention?

Consolidate and repackage the bundle of wands in the "now" and "later" piles. Leave the wands in the "never" or "discard" pile (other people's problems) behind. You can burn them in an imaginary bonfire, or actually write their problems on pieces of paper and burn them. Watch them disintegrate into ashes. Feel the peace and freedom from this gesture.

Place the "later" pile in a safe place—a cabinet, a chest, or inside a tree in your imagination. Finalize the practice by carrying the remaining wands easily in an appropriate container. Visualize yourself confidently striding toward your future holding the choices of personal responsibility in a carefree and mature manner.

This is an empowering meditation. It helps you realize that you have choices about the responsibilities and beliefs you carry, and the right to decide their priority in your life.

Five of Cups

The theme utilized for the Five of Cups meditation is faith in the future. The meditation allows you to grieve and then move beyond hopelessness to confidence in the belief in a new beginning. The river of life that flows through the scene is a reminder to stay in the flow and not become stagnant, for change has come and will come again. The bridge in the background suggests the possibility of passage from one situation to a different hope-filled future. The guidance is to surrender your attachment to negative emotions; don't let them become your identity.

A reorientation toward fulfillment of future desires is helpful; therefore consider performing a reading using a timeline of three to twelve months and emphasize the positive cards that appear in the spread. This will refocus you onto the upright Cups rather than on the ones that have already been spilt.

This meditation involves a release. It utilizes the spiritual significance of the upright and spilt cups depicted in the card in a releasing ceremony. The practice is designed to eliminate emotional bonds and desires that cause stagnation, disempowerment, and attraction of the same emotional situations. When you perceive the flow with hopeful new beliefs, you reclaim your personal assets, potentials, and a deeper awareness of your resources.

For the practice, you will need two special chalices or glasses, fresh, clean water, some blessed water, and a candle, paper, and pen. To prepare for the meditation, decide which emotional condition you want to release. This may be an attachment to suffering, an unproductive relationship, or past sorrows. Your choice should only involve the releasing of the unwanted feelings, not the banishment of a person. On a small piece of paper, write down the emotional burden you want to dissolve, then burn the paper and gather the ashes in a small container.

Imagine that you are in the scene presented in the Five of Cups. Note the flowing river, feel the heaviness of the mourning cloak, and then ultimately focus on the spilled cups. Visualize yourself setting the three spilled cups upright. See yourself placing the ashes of your banishing into one of them. Pour your grief and the emotional pain associated with the banishing into another of the three cups. Leave the third cup open for the entrance and movement of the spiritual power of forgiveness, cleansing, and the dissolution of grief.

Now focus your attention on the third, unfilled chalice; imagine it filled with sacred water—holy water, blessed water, or water treated with healing properties. See it filled with the sacred water of healing and dissolution; pour some into the other two chalices of sorrow. Witness the dissolving of all the energy held in these emotional containers. Gather all three cups, take them to the river, and cast them into it. Watch the contents float away; feel the release of the emotions. Do not judge; just let them all go. Slowly, come out of the meditative state feeling cleansed. Take the ashes from your banishment and flush them down the drain.

Now concentrate on the two special chalices and name them Love and Faith. Fill them with pure water, blessed water, or water treated with healing elixirs—Bach flower elixirs, or crystal and/or color drops with essential properties from your metaphysical store or health and wellness center. This will facilitate the harmonious vibration you wish to integrate.

Visualize a pink light of faith turning the water that color in one cup, representing personal self-love and healing. Picture a five-petaled rose in the cup. See blue water in the other cup, symbolizing faith in universal love and healing. Drink the water from both cups and affirm that you are loved and loving, and are in perfect harmony and flow with all sweetness and abundance in life. Know that this gesture of in-drinking affirms your faith in Divinity's constant flow of abundance, new life, and hope.

THREE OF SWORDS

The Three of Swords depicts a dramatic heart pierced by three swords. Although the wounds are distinct and evident, the heart is not shattered. No one leaves this life unscathed. It is what you opt to do with your wounds that determines your happiness and life path. You can allow them to define you, or you can choose to become strong at the wounded places.

This meditation begins with a visualization or actual visit to a place of divine love—a favorite natural setting, a healing temple, a sanctuary, or a chapel. Once you are comfortably seated in the location and have performed your deep breathing and relaxation, envision and request the presence of your Healer from the spiritual dimensions. This entity or power usually makes its presence felt at your left side; the traditional color of light it appears within is blue or blue-green. You can also call upon a healing archetype like the Archangels Michael (Temperance), Raphael (The Lovers), Gabriel (Judgement), or Uriel (The Hermit). Become firmly ensconced in the place or imagine yourself within the healing location and allow ample time to feel well-situated.

Focus your mind and breathing at your heart center. Know this is where the pain of love is stored, as well as the renewal of transformation and healing. After a few minutes, experience the sword representing your wound. You may choose to define the wound, or simply trust that the healing aspect of your Higher Self will remove all unnecessary pain and toxins that prevent wholeness. Imagine the sorrow leaving the wound (waves of emotion may be released).

See and feel the spiritual healing hand of your Healer as it removes the sword or swords from your heart area. Stay focused on your heart by breathing deeply and rhythmically. Flow with the images that come to you; flow with pain and feeling in order to recognize the block and release it. Bless the pain that may surface in feelings, thoughts, or memories. It has taught you much and some of the positive traits you have developed have come from its source. Allow ample time for this experience.

Flood the chamber of your heart with the healing color of light and with a magnified feeling of unconditional love from your Healer. Dissolve your attachment to the wound and feel its heaviness lift out of your heart. One way to facilitate healing is to visualize white light filling and sealing the space and cleansing the wound. Conclude by washing your heart area with purifying gold light.

End the meditation by affirming that your physical, emotional, and spiritual heart now beats in attunement with love, compassion, and wholeness. Repeat twice if necessary.

SEVEN OF SWORDS

The Seven of Swords meditation is for remedying self-betrayal. The practice will reveal the belief that fuels the betrayal. After breathing and relaxation, ask yourself the following questions or have a trusted person take on the role of interviewer.

- What aspect of me is not fully committed to myself?

- How does this lack of commitment reflect my upbringing?

- How do I repeat this pattern in my own actions and thoughts?

- Where do I take power away from myself?

- To whom do I give it?

- How does this disempowering thought reinforce my false, separated beliefs?

- What needs, feelings, or desires have I cut off?

- How do I deceive myself and others?

- Where do I owe myself an apology?

- What credit, recognition, validation, and appreciation do I owe myself?

These questions are highly valuable to consider and require insight and honesty on your part. The reward, however, is worth the effort involved. Think about how you can alter your attitude and beliefs to align truth with your self-worth. How can you treat yourself with the dignity you deserve? This is a time when consulting with a therapist may help show you a way to develop healthier behaviors. Self-help psychology books and biographies of those who have struggled with your specific turmoil are also beneficial.

Study the various Swords of power attributed to the triumph Sword cards in this section. Decide which one is appropriate for remedying the thoughts you've uncovered through this process of questioning. Visualize this particular sword of power and see it in front of you. When your sense of the sword is clearly felt, see the white, blue, or gold light emblazoning the blade with the specific aspect with which you've chosen to align yourself—the Sword of Peace, Mercy, Faith, etc. See the corresponding card in detail. Now envision your name also emblazoned on the sword, then place its image into your mind, your heart, and/or your entire being.

Finalize the practice by placing the corresponding card in a location you can easily see and use it as a focal point for daily meditation or affirmation, before falling asleep and upon waking.

EIGHT OF SWORDS

The purpose of this exercise is to liberate yourself from false beliefs. Choose to meditate on this card when you feel imprisoned by unwanted thoughts, beliefs, behaviors, or an external circumstance. The bondage illustrated in the card represents emotions and thoughts that are the ties that bind, which create restriction and enslavement to another's needs or self-limiting thoughts. You may feel obliged to keep your feelings locked inside. The bond that requires this kind of silence needs exploring and exposing, for the bond has become bondage.

In the card, a woman stands immobile, captured by circumstances, blinded by fear, bound and tied by attachments. Although the ground beneath her is murky, she could use her legs and feet to move out of her predicament. The forces that hold her catch her in a web of immobilization, but all will change and she will find release. The Eight of Swords involves fearful thinking and invasive domination from other's thoughts and controlling behavior. This predicament creates a weak mental and emotional stance.

The perceived external interference usually represents an internal power leak symbolized by the placement of the bonds around the torso where the lower three chakras of survival versus self-actualization, sexuality, and power/emotions are located. Note specifically where the ties end, your heart and upper chakras are free. The blindfold signals your lack of awareness and impeded vision, since you cannot see what you are not ready to understand.

Your body's instincts may be toward freedom, positive actions, and honoring the pure existence of your true liberated self, but your mind restricts the instinct's desire, creating a state of imprisonment. Both the thinking and the actions become fearful, inert, and limited. Somehow, you have lost or forfeited your power, or had it stolen. Perform this empowerment exercise to form a new accord between instinct, mind, emotion, and action.

When an initiate enters the mystery teachings, he or she is blindfolded and bound. This is a symbolic representation of the limitations imposed when you are restricted to the material, ego-based, and psychological self, in contrast to your greater self and life in the Spirit. The lesson's intention teaches that your lack of self-knowledge creates ignorance and stuck patterns of existence. Your emotional habits bind you as well; you can become a prisoner within your own psyche.

If the actual enactment of this meditation feels too daunting, use visualization instead. If at all possible, have another person ask the questions and guide the journey to empowerment and the breaking of the chains that bind.

Place yourself in a safe space where you won't be interrupted and enlist a trusted friend who understands the purpose of this practice. Choose a specifically troublesome area on which to focus for this exercise. Feel the emotions involved and speak the dilemma out loud to your friend. No judgment should be passed. Your body contains and stores information of which your intellect is unaware, or that is blocked from your knowing.

Have your friend blindfold you with a scarf, then bind your arms if this feels appropriate, as in the illustration. Or simply place your arms in a tight grasp against your body. Repeat the words and experience the emotional energies again. Of what does this feeling remind you?

Observe how you perceive the situation now that you are physically experiencing the limitation in personal power and strength. Speak your feelings to your friend; allow instinct—what you body wants to do (your lower torso, legs, and feet)—to guide your movement. Then follow your gut, perform the movements, and note your response.

What do your gestures tell your mind as movement occurs? Observe and speak to your friend. Does it remind you of your situation? Your past? How? Describe and take note. You may not have connected the two areas, but your body and gut "know" and now have an opportunity to teach you.

Remain in this state, then allow yourself to speak and ask for what you need. Note who you think can fulfill this need; realize this is who or what you have been bonded to and that you desire release and liberation. Now ask yourself for your needs to be fulfilled. Repeat your name and say: "I need this from you."

On a prearranged signal, have your friend ask your arms and hands to show you what you need to do to free yourself. Speak and do. Allow time for realization to come up, vocalize again, and notice how you move your hands and arms. Now what does it feel like? What memories are evoked? Allow your instinct to guide your response. Follow up this exercise with a discussion about action and consciousness, asking what to do and exploring an attitude that will help you facilitate growth.

Your legs and feet represent strength from a positive support system of personal beliefs that ground you and direct you onto an improved, liberated path. What do they want to do now that they are free? Look for readiness, fortitude, and open-mindedness; ask for guidance and help and new uses for your imagination. Especially look for concepts connected with taking a stand and understanding what is needed for the creation of movement. Ask your support person to record your feelings and thoughts.

The release of that which binds you is the final, closing step in this odyssey. Start by acknowledging the person or condition at the source of the disturbance, then feel the emotions, frustrations, and confusions. Develop one word or short sentence that represents your held-back, limited self. For example, if what you are afraid of limits your life experience, that emotion, anger, grief, or hurt can be healed by allowing the emotion to come up and be released through expression.

Name it and claim it. Then bind the influence by visualizing the person and the emotion. Now picture a netting falling completely over them or over the scene of the trauma; they are held fast, sealed and captured by the netting. Cast the net completely out to the universal light so that, if more light is to come to the person, it will be done, ensuring they can no longer harm you. Bid them farewell and tell them to go in peace. End the meditation by recalling the need you previously expressed and affirming that the need is now fulfilled by the universe.

NINE OF SWORDS

This meditation is based on the old adage that an old rose disintegrates and a new one blooms. The meditation follows a rose through its natural evolution; it blooms, withers, and dies. Obtain a single rose. Name the rose as the belief system that no longer serves you—something you can determine through studying the exercise for the Seven of Swords. Each day, as you watch the rose age, know this is symbolic of your old, negative desires passing away.

After the bloom has withered, take the dry petals and burn them, while declaring yourself free of hurtful desires. Become aware of the fear of detaching from identification with this attitude and release the fear as you burn the petals. Remember, the red rose symbolizes life's pleasures and passions, and the desires of the heart. The rose, with its yellow background, stems (all puns intended) from The Magician's rosebush, and the color theme repeats in the Strength trump. The Arcanum represents the power and lesson of loving, and of natural desires. Where there was once desire for destruction or power-mongering, replace it with a better desire—for example, for peace. Passionately wanting true love, lasting prosperity, and spiritual purposefulness requires trust, faith, and an open heart on your part. Expand the realm of your desires, and make sure they are the highest, most authentic, soulful ones you can imagine—filled with deservedness and not hampered by "cross-purposes" or beliefs in undeservedness.

Place The Magician and the Strength card in front of you and ask for guidance about redesigning a new desire that is just and true. As you design a program of affirmation and visualization using the two cards, a change occurs from helplessness to self-help, from which compatible actions and attitudes will develop. As you practice these, they will become tools of adaptation from a destructive to a constructive self.

Finalize the practice by obtaining a permanent symbol of your oath to allow perfect fulfillment of your deepest, most self-loving desires. Sometimes, the purchase and wearing of a symbolic new ring, necklace, or bracelet is appropriate. Rose quartz is the stone associated to heartfelt desires; emerald and peridot heal and vivify the heart chakra.

A living plant or a rosebush that will bloom every year, reminding you of the essence and embodiment of your oath to fulfill your desires, is also an appropriate token of your blooming, genuine desires.

Note for Astrologers

For astrologers, examine transits or progression aspects of a challenging nature—in other words, take note of squares and oppositions for a predictive time frame regarding the card's crisis. Adjustments will be required as repeated conflicts test you to bring mastery over the unconscious and your planets. Additionally, look at your natal chart's challenging aspects again, including squares, T-squares, grand squares, and opposition, as these may be involved with energies surrounding the appearance of this card.

Note the emphasis on the square and T-square in the card's composition in the Waite deck. The zodiac sigils hint at astrological consideration. When contending with the challenge quality of the T-square, look to the sign of the missing side of the square as the way out or as a way to integrate the conflicting energies. For example, if the missing sign on a mutable T-square is Gemini, then communicating that sign's attribute is the way to resolve the situation. If the T-square is in fixed signs and Taurus is missing, practicality and security are the way to go. A square asks you to consider conflicting ways of doing things, of reflecting values and aptitudes. You must stand strong in the higher expression of your Sun sign and integrate the spiritual qualities. See the Sun card for your zodiacal strength.

TEN OF SWORDS

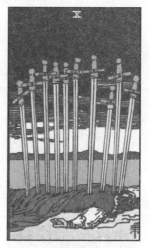

This meditation works to release the emotions and beliefs connected to life's failures and grief. It utilizes the spiritual property of water—that of cleansing and renewal. This is available to you, as suggested by the shoreline scene as well as the symbolic sunrise depicted on the card. Water always promises flow, union, healing, and new life.

Choose your favorite watery location—a favorite beach, river, ocean, lake, or waterfall—to visit or visualize for the practice. Place yourself, like the card's character, by the water's edge, and imagine the darkness of storm clouds hanging above you. Picture yourself as you were, or are, when experiencing fear, despair, or defeat. Allow yourself to feel the emotions. Be aware of the negative message accompanying the experience. For example: "I am a worthless human being," or "I am too _____ to have _____." Also look at the conscious rationalization you have adopted—your denial, your defense system, your excuses, and the blaming that supports that fear or failure—for they must be cleansed from you too.

Now move into the water in any way that you feel comfortable. These are baptismal waters, taking you to your renewal. Feel the water cleanse you. Affirm you are being washed clean from all unnecessary fear and pain about failure—past, present, and future. Allow the water to move around and within you, dissolving and disintegrating your old self.

As this occurs, feel the gold and pink of sunrise fill the scene and your entire being. Focus particularly on your heart center, the place where transformation occurs. Wash the center with the pink of unconditional love and the gold of spiritual will. Know that you have offered up and surrendered the old condition to the sea of universal understanding. Complete your renewal with prayer and the invocation of a new affirmation as you return to shore.

Know, as each day passes, that the Sun, symbolic of your new self, will rise, attain power, recede, and reliably rise again.

FIVE OF PENTACLES

The challenge in the Five of Pentacles is to reconnect with the spiritual source. Charity, understood as giving oneself to divine beneficence and subsequently allowing this gift to flow through you, is imperative for rescuing the card's couple. The card's setting of destitute characters passing underneath a blazing church window indicates the need to tend to spiritual values. The impoverished people symbolize the alienated, unenlightened aspects within you. A destitute female leads a disabled male in the wintry scene. This indicates that subconscious beliefs (the female is symbolically associated with soul, emotions, the psyche, and the subconscious), both positive and negative, are in charge. The male traditionally symbolizes the function of reason and assertion. In this card, they are both impaired, yet drawn to the light beaming from the window.

The idea of this meditation is to understand that these un-evolved characters exist within you and are in need of light, warmth, healing, and transmutation. The contrast between light and dark is dramatic in the picture, and the scene is set for a realization derived from "bottoming out," or the dark night of the soul.

Choose a particular aspect of your life that makes you feel like the characters of the card—i.e., suffering, isolation, impoverishment, weakness, or alienation from your desires. Great healing and reunion needs to occur in this area through an acceptance of worthiness, deservedness, and allowance of blessing and unification with the charity of Spirit.

Imagine yourself outdoors in inhospitable, cold, snowy conditions; this icy state suggests frozen emotional or subconscious conditioning. A cathedral or temple stands before you. Feel all the physical elements—the sensation of going barefoot in the wet, cold, howling wind, snow falling, and the inadequacy of your clothing.

Ask yourself what these feelings recall from your past. This may be represented as a traumatic memory, a specific event, a feeling, or a visual image of painful memories. What is revealed may not seem recognizable and connected to the issue you have chosen to understand. Accept what "comes up" and then ask for further clarity. The conditions around the memory or feeling may come from your recent or remote past. How did this earlier event or first presentation of memory make you feel? Understand that you have cloaked yourself in this suffering, wearing it as a garment that is, in reality, unfitting and poorly constructed, and that represents a negative self-image. Summarize this insight into your negative self as a formula: love = hurt = mistrust; poor health = attention = comfort and security, etc.

Shift your awareness to the beautiful stained-glass window and stand in its colored glow. Note the hues and design. Sense the light's warmth; feel it reach out to you and pour through you to cleanse and vivify your auric field. Now allow the old mantle of impoverished beliefs and negativity to drop away and melt into the snow. Continue to fill yourself with light, knowing spiritual light is a representation of the Divine. Allow the lighted window to enlarge and encompass you, until all walls and barriers are removed and there are no obstacles between you and your illuminated self. Dedicate and commit your transformed self to the healing, forgiveness, and divine love that is always available.

Now see yourself as the woman in a clean white garment, filled with hope and radiating a new light of love to others. Feel the temperature rise; the snow is melting and the scent of spring is in the air. Move toward the male character, embrace him, and help him walk into the light shed by the window. Feel the union between you and the healed, transformed male and female. Experience yourself as one with the light radiating from the window; become that light.

The characters descend from the light. The male stands upright; he has no need of crutches, and he is filled with light, hope, and new life. Understand that he is your masculine side, the part of you that reasons and takes you out into the world. He is now strong and works in partnership with the new female spirituality. She is the one who holds the vision he will act upon, so her beliefs must be whole and aligned with her highest good. Ask that your new union with divine grace, Providence, and abundance guide all thoughts and healing actions in daily life.

Create a strong visualization and affirmation, perhaps using some of the elements experienced in the window of light. Think of this vision in the present tense; pulse it with light from the divine and repeat your affirmation during walks or other physical activities, since the movement helps to ground and embody your intent. Regard this practice as your daily prayer, or time spent in the temple.

CONCLUSION

Synchronicity, or "co-incidental" experiences, are part of the intrigue of living with the energies of the Tarot for me. Its influence has served as an inspirational winged messenger throughout my waking and dreaming life—sometimes predictive, often surprising and Fool-like, and always profound.

In August of 1987, when my art college offered an off-campus program in Florence, Italy, I applied and was accepted. Little did I know what the spirits of the Tarot had planned for me. One day, soon after our group's arrival, I was walking through the beautifully preserved Renaissance streets, juxtaposed with modern marble facades of contemporary designer's showrooms, when I came across a colorful poster of a painting featuring a Renaissance version of the Tarot's Magician card. "Amministrazione Provinciale de Ferrara presents Le Carte Di Corte, I Tarrochi Gioco E Maglia alla Corte degli Estensi." Unbeknownst to me, a once-in-a-lifetime Tarot exhibition was to take place precisely during the period of my school year—a major coincidence.

Here was a rare opportunity to see actual surviving fifteenth-century hand-painted Tarot cards that were in collections worldwide, now returned to the castle where they were first presented to the Court. Original Tarot cards from that era to 1944 were available for viewing, along with contemporary artists' versions of the cards that included a larger-than-life Hermit's lantern and a fountain created to represent the Temperance card. For me, the symbolic, experiential, and artistic aspects of the Tarot have been very meaningful, so the forces of synchronicity made sure I visited this grand exposition.

My dream life often predicts the future and offers insight to me using the Tarot. When I began writing this volume, I dreamt of the last card in the Major Arcana series, The World card. The mandorla wreath's leaves had become roses that were budding, and I was inside the wreath. When I finished writing the book, I had another dream. Here is what I wrote in my dream journal. "I dreamed of my future flying toward me today. It was in the form of a monarch butterfly. It repeatedly flew at me until its orange wings caught my attention; it came from the right-hand side, the future. I knew the butterfly represented The Fool."

APPENDIX I

CARD THEMES

A Note about Card Themes

This section will give you a quick reference to the essence of each card in the Major Arcana as well as the relevant keywords for each suit in the Minor Arcana. As you work with the tarot, keep in mind the following regarding direction of the card:

Upright cards:
The principle represented is functioning harmoniously.

Reversed:
There is difficulty with the specific theme represented by the card or suit.

MAJOR ARCANA

The Fool
*Positive leap of faith,
spiritual destiny*

The Magician
Focus on best intention

The High Priestess
*Treat the situation with sacredness; a
soul mystery*

The Empress
Radiant love; power of attraction

The Emperor
*Manifestation of destiny; destined
manifestation*

The Hierophant
*Hearing and listening to intuition
and teacher*

The Lovers

Healing; correct choice-making; loving relationships

The Chariot

Soul self; successes, triumphs

Strength

Courage and self-care

The Hermit

Wisdom and attainment

Wheel of Fortune
Beneficent cycle; opening to receive goodness

Justice
Balance, righteousness, new cycle, adjustment

The Hanged Man
Surrender control; rest in faith

Death
Liberation; endings, beginnings

Temperance

Moderation, modification, adaptation

The Devil

Facing fears

The Tower

Realization; waking up

The Star

True self and purpose

The Moon

Subconscious, instinct, psychic

The Sun

Protection; spiritual radiance

Judgement

Release of past; reunion with the soul

The World

Attainment and completion

SUITS

WANDS
Courage; strength, will aspiration

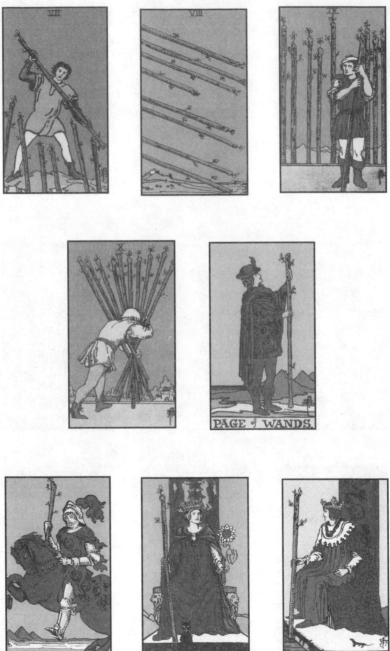

Cups

Faith and love

SWORDS

Justice; just rewards; constructive thought and action

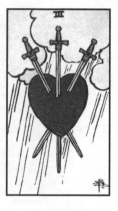

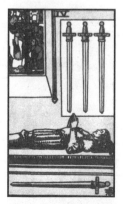

PENTACLES

Charity, beneficence; labors of love; work, service and monetary matters

PAGE OF PENTACLES

KNIGHT OF PENTACLES

QUEEN OF PENTACLES

KING OF PENTACLES

QUICK GUIDE
TO THE
TAROT SPREADS

The Celtic Cross Spread

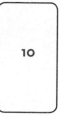

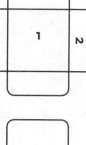

Indicator Card
Position 1, Present Influence
Position 2, Helps and Hindrances
Position 3, The Past Foundation
Position 4, Recent Event
Position 5, Possible Future
Position 6, Immediate Future
Position 7, Attitude
Position 8, Environment and Others
Position 9, Hopes and Fears
Position 10, Final Outcome

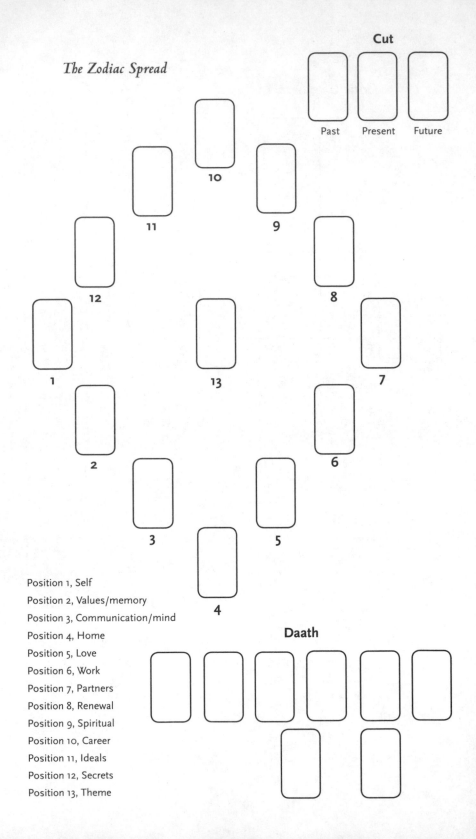

The Zodiac Spread

Cut

Past   Present   Future

10

11   9

12   8

1   13   7

2   6

3   5

4

Position 1, Self
Position 2, Values/memory
Position 3, Communication/mind
Position 4, Home
Position 5, Love
Position 6, Work
Position 7, Partners
Position 8, Renewal
Position 9, Spiritual
Position 10, Career
Position 11, Ideals
Position 12, Secrets
Position 13, Theme

Daath

The Whole Self Spread

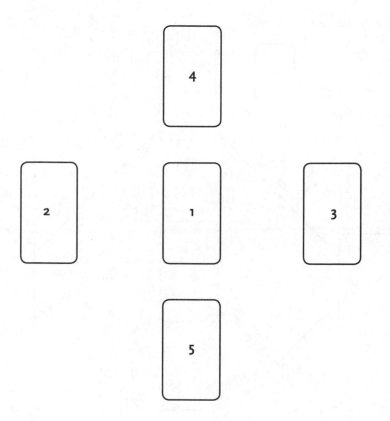

Position 1, Essence, theme, energy involved in the matter
Position 2, The ego, conscious attitude, who you think you are
Position 3, Subconscious powers, the subconscious, who you may not
       know yourself to be
Position 4, Intuition, challenges, lessons
Position 5, The physical action

The Four Seasons Spread

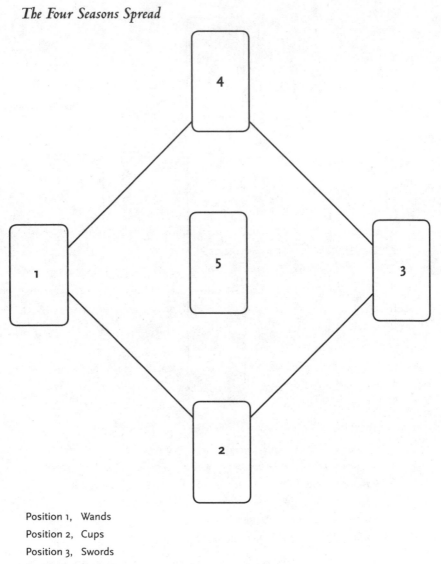

Position 1, Wands
Position 2, Cups
Position 3, Swords
Position 4, Pentacles
Position 5, Major Arcana

WHY WE READ
THE TAROT

*B*est *Tarot Practices* is dedicated to all readers of the Tarot. I asked
my colleagues and students to share their answers to the essential question all Tarot readers ponder at some point: "Why do you
read the cards?" Their answers were unique, ranging from inspirational to practical, and they mentioned the benefits of building
self-awareness, social connections, and relationships. I feel their
comments reflect the value of being a Tarot reader.

"I believe that my purpose in this lifetime is to plant the seeds of knowl-
edge and divine light in as many people as I can possibly reach. When
you plant a seed of insight, of understanding, of possibility, its natural
instinct is to grow. Through my Tarot readings I am able to plant many,
many seeds. My workshops, classes and private consultations give people
the power to take control of their lives and create their own inner peace
and happiness."

—E.J.B., Buffalo, New York

"The positive side of the Tarot for me is that the cards show you the
innermost state of your psyche: where the problem is and where you have
to start to change something. The same cards will appear consistently in
readings, especially when you read them for yourself. The Ten of Swords

followed me for years until I finally understood its meaning and began to do something about it in my head and, subsequently, my life.

I use the Tarot to monitor my progress and find out if I am really on the way to a more positive outlook or if I am kidding myself. I use the Celtic Cross Spread for myself with the simple question, "Where am I at the moment?" This always gives me good insight into my own way of thinking and the energies around me. The Tarot is an invaluable tool in your quest for a better life."

—E.J., Munich, Germany

"When one reads the Tarot, the world comes to you. I have met so many people of various cultures, lifestyles, and careers that I have learned from—things I never would have known so deeply without connecting with them through their personal experiences using the Tarot."

—B.D., Winnipeg, Manitoba , Canada

"The most meaningful experience that has happened (and still happens to this day) is more around my personal use of the cards, as opposed to reading for other people. It seems that the cards become "real" and sort of take on a life of their own as vivid symbols in some clairvoyant experience. It is as if the characters are communicating with me in person. The most memorable example of this was when I was in a job interview. Near the end of the interview, the hand from the Ace of Cups appeared and hovered between the interviewer and me. The hand reached out and tied a beautiful silver cord in a knot, and right then I knew that I had gotten the job. When this started happening, I realized that my clairvoyant ability was using the cards as a vehicle."

—T.E., Toronto, Ontario, Canada

ACKNOWLEDGMENTS

Thank you to The Emperor, Joseph G. Schick, my life partner, for his strength, love, and support.

Thank you to The Hermit, Patrick Crean, for holding up his lantern of light so I could see the vision of this book.

Deep gratitude to The High Priestess, Ellen Bourn, for her spiritual companionship and to The Queen of Wands, Carole Tolley, for her metaphysical mind that helped to shape the contents.

I am honored by the kind words that Rachel Pollack wrote in her introduction, thank you.

Sincere appreciation also goes to Brenda Knight, Sandi Matuschka, Josee Ledoux, Carolyn Olive, Chris DeGrow, and Donna Van Toen for their efforts to bring this book to fruition.

ABOUT THE AUTHOR

Marcia Masino is a Certified Grand-master of Tarot, as awarded by the The American Tarot Association. She is the author of the Tarot classic *Easy Tarot Guide*. She has lectured at numerous Tarot conferences and is a popular speaker for The Lily Dale Assembly workshop program. Her articles on metaphysical subjects have appeared in *Fate Magazine* and on the web at *Stariq.com*. She lives in Pickering, Ontario, Canada. Her website is *marciamasinotarotshop.org*.